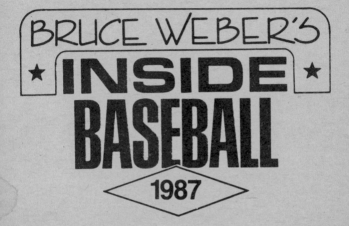

BRUCE WEBER'S
★ INSIDE ★
BASEBALL
1987

D0775627

SCHOLASTIC INC.
New York Toronto London Auckland Sydney

Scholastic Books are available at special discounts for quantity purchases for use as premiums, promotional items, retail sales through specialty market outlets, etc. For details contact: Special Sales Manager, Scholastic Inc., 730 Broadway, New York, NY 10003.

ISBN 0-590-40798-8

Copyright © 1987 by Scholastic Books, Inc. All rights reserved. Published by Scholastic Inc.

12 11 10 9 8 7 6 5 4 3 2   7 8 9/8 0 1 2/9

Printed in the U.S.A.   01

First Scholastic printing, March 1987

CONTENTS

1987: A Look Ahead   **1**

American League All-Pro Team   **5**

National League All-Pro Team   **17**

American League Team Previews   **29**

National League Team Previews   **59**

Statistics 1986   **85**

   American League Batting   **86**

   American League Pitching   **93**

   National League Batting   **96**

   National League Pitching   **103**

Bruce Weber Picks How They'll Finish
   in 1987   **107**

You Pick How They'll Finish
   in 1987   **108**

If 1987 is Mike Schmidt's last year, the Phils' future Hall-of-Fame third sacker wants to make it a pennant-winning one.

1987: A Look Ahead

With east coast World Series games starting in the middle of the evening and finishing in early morning, Series visitors get plenty of chances to tour historic sights and eat in slow-paced restaurants. We found lots of both in Boston last fall, though we doubt we can use that knowledge again this year.

Despite Roger Clemens, Jim Rice, solid Rich Gedman, pesky Marty Barrett, and the rest of the Sox, a repeat World Series just doesn't appear in the cards. (It doesn't appear in the cards for the Cards, either.) Fact is, the AL East is loaded; it's the strongest division in the game. If the starting pitching improves and the bullpen holds up, the Yankees will be stronger. The Indians are coming, the Orioles can't be that bad, and the Blue Jays are extremely tough. Detroit and Milwaukee are in the hunt, too. A repeat division title by the Bosox would be most impressive.

Despite recent history — division champs, much less league and world champs, don't repeat — we're going with the Mets again in '87. You'll find our illogical logic explained elsewhere in these pages. Basically, we believe the Mets have too much talent that has not yet been fully used. We doubt that Bob Ojeda will go 18–5 again or that Roger McDowell will win 14 games, coming out of the bullpen. There is some room for improvement, and GM Frank Cashen and manager Davey Johnson will coax it out.

A Met repeat in the NL East will not come nearly as easily as the '86 breeze. A healthy Hubie Brooks will make a difference in Montreal, if the other pieces of the Expo puzzle are back in place. (Free agency: Isn't it wonderful?) The Phillies are a solid offensive team, the Cardinals have to bounce back, and even the Cubs and Bucs should be a little better.

Youngsters wearing Giants and Reds uniforms should tighten things up in the NL West, where the "death" of the Dodgers was one of the bigger stories of '86. If Houston finds another power source to go with Glenn Davis, there's no telling what they can do. But the final championship series games raised some questions about their bullpen. The Reds are probably a mite closer to victory than the Giants, but both should be fun to watch for years to come. Neither the Padres nor the Braves look to be ready to challenge for the top spot. Both, however, have some great talent.

Houston's 1986 victory could inspire the Texas Rangers in the AL West. After the I–70 Series between the Cards and Royals in 1985 and the I–95 Series between the Red Sox and Mets in 1986, manager Bobby Valentine's Rangers are hoping for an I–45 Series in '87. That's the road that links the Rangers' Dallas-Fort-Worth-area home with Houston. Stranger things have happened. If Valentine can change the strike-out-walk situation (more strikeouts and fewer walks by his pitchers, the reverse for his young sluggers), it could be the Rangers' year.

The Angels are the least likely of last year's play-off teams to repeat. The Royals have the tools to bounce back, the Athletics are coming on, and the White Sox and Mariners can't help but improve. As usual, the AL West will be interesting.

Getting down to serious business, like where to eat dinner next October, National League fans will get to enjoy the many great restaurants in New York and the wonderful German eateries in Cincinnati. AL fans will divide the play-offs between some great chili in Texas and the mid-October chill in Toronto. The Series? It's back to the highway, New York's Dewey Thruway from New York City to Buffalo, then the Queensway to Toronto. Anyone with Toronto restaurant suggestions?

— Bruce Weber

December 15, 1986

No pitcher has ever won the Cy Young and MVP awards two straight years. But Boston's Roger Clemens feels he has a shot.

American League ALL-PRO TEAM

First Base
DON MATTINGLY
NEW YORK YANKEES

He's only 25 years old, going on 26 in late April. He's been a major-leaguer for just four seasons. He didn't even win the AL's MVP Award despite incredible numbers in '86. Yet there probably isn't a manager around who wouldn't make Donald Arthur Mattingly his first choice if he were starting a new team.

The man from Indiana does it all for New York (the Bronx, at least). The 6–0, 175-pounder, who was born and raised in Evansville, IN, owns a nearly perfect swing. He combines great natural talent with an amazing capacity to work. He's good at hitting because he works hard at it. And his defense is right up there with his Met rival, Keith Hernandez, the standard by which first sackers are measured.

In 1985 Don led the AL in RBIs, doubles, and sacrifice flies. He was among the leaders in a bunch of other categories. In '86 he was even better. He hit .352 (second to Wade Boggs's .357), led in doubles (53, topping Lou Gehrig's all-time Yankee mark), led in hits (238, topping Earle Combs's all-time Yankee mark), knocked in 113 runs, smacked 31 homers, led the league in slugging (.573), and more. Our choice for MVP? Sorry, Roger. It's Don.

TONY BERNAZARD
CLEVELAND INDIANS

For those of you who have been waiting for Tony Bernazard, your wait is over. The 29-year-old from Caguas, Puerto Rico, has spent six seasons in the majors, in both leagues. And now he's among the best.

It would have been easy to give up on Bernazard. Several teams did. He spent part of two seasons with the Montreal Expos, then arrived in the bigs to stay with the White Sox in 1981. A couple of seasons later he was dealt to Seattle. Finally, in 1984, he arrived in Cleveland, where he has found a home.

There was a flash in 1984. He opened the season hitting .390, then went 0-for-44 and slumped to .221. Awful. After a .274 season in '85, it all came together last year. And what year! A lifetime .255 hitter, Tony cracked the ball at a .301 pace, easily his biggest major-league season. And he combined with shortstop Julio Franco to give the up-rising Tribe tremendous strength up the middle.

Tony also racked up career highs in homers (17), RBIs (73), and hits (169). And now, after 12 years as a professional, six in the minors and six in the majors, Antonio Bernazard is where he wants to be: on top.

Third Base
WADE BOGGS
BOSTON RED SOX

Wade Boggs's critics have always carped, "So he hits singles. So what?" Critics take note: Wade Boggs is a complete player. Maybe he doesn't hit with much power. But his glove is first-rate, and he can hurt you in a variety of ways. He's an All-Pro.

New York fans may accuse Boggs of beating Don Mattingly of the Yanks for the batting title (.357 to .352) by sitting out the final games of the season. But there's no questioning Boggs's ability with the bat. His career mark of .353 places him among the all-timers. Look at his batting average for each of the past five years: .349, .361, .325, .368, and .357. In '86, despite missing 13 games (because of the death of his mother and assorted injuries), he still racked up 207 hits (career total: 979), 47 doubles (second to Mattingly's 53), and a .401 on-base percentage.

Though Mattingly is probably the best all-around hitter in the game, Boggs has the better chance to become the next .400 hitter. He's a hard worker. ("He's always the first player at the ball park," says manager John McNamara.) And he's a real student of hitting. He owns one of the most beautiful strokes in the game. And he's its best third baseman, too.

Shortstop
TONY FERNANDEZ
TORONTO BLUE JAYS

The American League has its share of excellent shortstops. There's young Julio Franco in Cleveland; Ozzie Guillen in Chicago; Alfredo Griffin in Oakland; and the boss's son, Cal Ripken, Jr., in Baltimore. But the main man this time is the fellow in Canada, Toronto's Tony Fernandez.

You can count on Fernandez. Though he plays in Toronto, his home is in the Dominican Republic. That island seems to breed great shortstops. Many of the top major-leaguers these days call the Dominican Republic home. But not many of them can match the lanky (6–2, 165-pound) Fernandez in all-around ability.

Although 1986 was his first .300-plus season, there has been little doubt about Tony's bat. Still, '86 was remarkable. He hit .310 to lead the Jays and finish seventh in the AL. He was third in hits (213) and triples (9); and set career highs in RBIs (65), homers (10, twice his previous career total!), doubles (33), and stolen bases (25).

At age 24, the owner of both a great bat and a super glove, Fernandez has a positively brilliant future. Combined with the Jays' great outfield, Fernandez and his mates are waiting for the pitching to catch up with the rest of the club. Then watch out!

9

Outfield
JIM
RICE
BOSTON RED SOX

Opening night of the 1986 World Series. The Met fan turns to his Red Sox counterpart. "I just hope," said the New Yorker, "that Jim Rice always comes to the plate with the bases empty." Basically, that's what happened. Billy Buckner, the Sox No. 3 hitter, didn't have a great Series (forget the Game 6 error), and Rice never hurt the Mets.

But fear — by Sox opponents — is Rice's game. After two seasons that Rice considered un-Ricelike, Jim became the old Rice again in '86. There's no reason to believe he won't continue in '87 and beyond.

Production is the key to Rice's success. As the Sox trooped to the 1986 AL title, it seemed that Jim was always banging in the key runs. After hitting .280 and .291 the previous two years, he returned to the AL's hitting aces last year, hitting .324, along with 110 RBIs and 39 doubles. He also had 20 homers and 12 game-winning RBIs. That's Jim Rice.

"I just go out there every day and try to do my job. That means knocking in runs," says the South Carolina native. "With our pitching, it doesn't take many runs."

"I wish I had more guys who 'just did their job' like Jim," says manager John McNamara. "He carries the club."

Outfield
KIRBY PUCKETT
MINNESOTA TWINS

What, people were asking early last season, is a Kirby Puckett? There are all sorts of clever answers, of course. But the folks in Minnesota know the real one. The compact Kirby Puckett — he's only 5–8 and weights 185 pounds — is one fine baseball player. Patrolling the middle of the outfield for the Twins in their homerdome, Puckett gets the job done at-bat and in the field. And how he gets it done!

If he played in a normal league (one without Wade Boggs and Don Mattingly), Puckett would have been right in the hunt for the 1986 AL batting title. As it was, he finished third with a none-too-shabby .328 mark. It came in the Chicago native's third big-league campaign, and raised his career average over the .300 mark for the first time.

The little powerhouse also cranked out 31 homers (helped by his home park), finished third in slugging (.537), second in runs scored (119), and second in hits (223).

None of this comes as any surprise to the Twin organization, which picked Puckett in the first round of the draft back in '82. He hit the big-time after only two-and-a-fraction minor-league seasons. This 25-year-old is super.

Outfield
GEORGE BELL
TORONTO BLUE JAYS

Toronto's George Bell decided to take a page from the notebook of all-time lefty Steve Carlton. No, he's not becoming a pitcher. He just doesn't talk to the press. That's a mistake, we believe. But as long as his bat keeps talking, Bell will have no major problems.

In Toronto's outstanding outfield, Bell stands out. Despite a slumbering September, the 27-year-old from the Dominican Republic had another great year. Though his late-season blues dropped his average from .330 to a final .309, he still finished ninth in the AL batting race. He also broke a club record for RBIs (108, tied with Jesse Barfield). Though he lacks Barfield's shotgun arm, he still scares AL base runners.

Jays manager Jimy Williams, who inserted Bell into the clean-up spot of the batting order full-time, has nothing but good things to say about Bell. "I don't know what else I can ask George to do," says the field boss. "He's the kind of player you enjoy sharing a dugout with."

All-Pro pickers are also advised to check out Barfield (.289, league-leading 40 homers, 108 RBIs, .559 slugging percentage, and 107 runs scored). What a pair of Jays!

12

Catcher
RICH GEDMAN
BOSTON RED SOX

Baseball — and the Red Sox — are like religion in New England. From April to October, "the Sawks" are everything. And though many folks "worship" the superstars like Roger Clemens and Jim Rice, those in the know realize that catcher Rich Gedman is a key man, day in and day out.

Their support is not without merit. The man they call "Geddy" plays a key position and plays it better than anyone in the AL. A good defensive catcher, he also threw out 44 of the 86 opponents who tried to steal on Boston pitchers last year. In addition, he's a potent force in Boston's big attack. At age 27, the local boy made good. (He was born in Worcester, MA.) He has made many Red Sox fans forget Carlton Fisk, the previous No. 1 Boston backstop. His only major problem is a series of nagging injuries that, at times, cause him problems on defense.

Meanwhile, the powerful 6–0, 215-pounder is one of the AL's tougher outs, despite a seemingly fair .258 average in 135 games in '86. But he swatted 16 homers and knocked in 65 runs, including six game-winners. He also hit .357 in the AL Championship Series, while managing a pitching staff that put the Red Sox into the World Series for the first time in 11 years.

13

Righthanded Pitcher
ROGER CLEMENS
BOSTON RED SOX

To the surprise of no one, Roger Clemens was the AL Cy Young Award winner for '86. To the surprise of a few, he won it unanimously. Roger smeared the Yanks' Don Mattingly and teammate Jim Rice in the AL MVP race. And as a result, the 24-year-old Clemens joins guys like Sandy Koufax and Bob Gibson as pitchers with combined Cy Young-MVP seasons.

Roger is worthy of the company. The 6–4, 205-pounder, who grew up deep in the heart of Texas, is the "stopper" every championship team needs. Fourteen of his victories followed Red Sox losses. With Clemens out there, the Sox were in little danger of falling into a real slump.

His 24–4 season matched Dwight Gooden's 1985 numbers, when everyone called Gooden the greatest thing since sliced bread. Roger's ERA was 2.48, easily the AL's best, and his 238 strikeouts placed him narrowly behind Seattle's Mark Langston. (Roger's final-week elbow injury may have cost him that title.)

Hard as it is to believe, Roger was once a Met draft choice. Fortunately for Sox fans, Roger decided to wait, which landed him smack in the middle of Fenway Park. He'll be there for years to come.

Lefthanded Pitcher
TEDDY HIGUERA
MILWAUKEE BREWERS

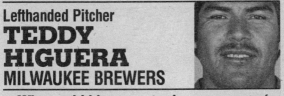

Who could blame major-league scouts for booking airline tickets to Mexico? If they're looking for lefthanded pitchers, that seems to be the place to look. The Dodgers' Fernando Valenzuela has been the NL's top southpaw for years. Now along comes the Brewers' Teddy Higuera, the first American Leaguer to win 20 for a losing team in a decade.

With a little more support, Higuera might have won even more, possibly challenging Boston's Roger Clemens for the Cy Young Award. Still, his 20 wins, 2.79 ERA (second in the league behind Clemens), and 207 strikeouts (sixth in the AL and a Milwaukee club record) produced a most satisfying season for the young lefty.

Higuera is a power pitcher, who earns his money by busting his fastball and keeping it down. And he's a master at hitting the corners. Down and in. Down and away. That made it easy for his personal catcher, Charlie Moore. "It was really easy for me," said Moore. "This kid is only going to get better."

"Face it," says 1986 Brewer manager (and pitching expert) George Bamberger, "Teddy's a great one. He has a brilliant future."

15

Master of the split-fingered fastball, Astro ace Mike Scott leads Houston on the trail of a second straight NL West title.

National League
ALL-PRO TEAM

First Base
KEITH HERNANDEZ
NEW YORK METS

The pro's pro. Mr. Consistency. Those are the labels fans hang on Keith Hernandez. Though Gary Carter got more attention, the first sacker might well have been the champs' Most Valuable Player in '86. He could well be again in '87.

Hernandez, a native of the San Francisco Bay Area, is a true artist. His bat work is magnificent. His .310 average in '86 followed seasons of .311 and .312. That, friends, is consistent. And his performance in the field is right out of the first baseman's textbook. When batting, most baseball teams take a sacrifice for granted. Get the bunt down, and the runner will move up. Not against the Mets and Hernandez. The lefty loves to swoop in, grab the ball, turn, and throw to second. He's incredible.

The one-time Cardinal star hit in some hard luck during the '86 World Series. He hit the ball on the nose almost every trip to the plate. But the ball usually headed toward a Red Sox. But when the Mets needed some punch in Game 7, there was Hernandez. His line single brought the Mets back from 3–0 to 3–2 on the way to their final 8–5 victory. That's Hernandez, the guy who gets the job done day after day.

Second Base
STEVE SAX
LOS ANGELES DODGERS

The National League is, to put it mildly, loaded at second base. St. Louis's Tommy Herr could well bounce back to his '85 form. Phillie Juan Samuel can hurt you so many ways. The Cubs' Ryne Sandberg and Pittsburgh's Johnny Ray are solid pros. The Giants' Robby Thompson is the second sacker of the future, and the Mets' pesty Wally Backman was a key to the world champs' title drive.

But our choice at second is the Dodgers' No. 1 hitman. That's Steve Sax, who hits the ball a ton and has overcome his woes in the field. Dodger fans are convinced that Tim Raines of the Expos won the 1986 NL bat title by sitting out the Expos' final game. Sax finished just out of the money with a .332 mark. (Raines hit .334.)

The one-time scatter-armed Sax also just missed on the hit title (210 to Tony Gwynn's 211), was second in doubles (43), and was tied for third in on-base percentage (.390), behind Raines and Keith Hernandez (.413 each).

That was a lot of production for manager Tom Lasorda, who saw his Dodgers finish ninth in the league in hitting. Better still, Sax played in 157 Dodger games, 24 more than the No. 2 guy, Franklin Stubbs.

Third Base
MIKE SCHMIDT
PHILADELPHIA PHILLIES

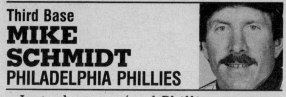

Just when you (and Phillies management) thought that Mike Schmidt had had it, the big banger from Ohio staged a tremendous comeback, becoming the NL's 1986 MVP. Only one year after being shifted to first base, the NL's top slugger returned to the hot corner. He quickly proved with bat and glove that he still owns the spot.

True, third base isn't the NL's best position. LA's Bill Madlock may be done. Montreal's Tim Wallach is good. Pittsburgh's Jim Morrison needs another great year to prove himself. And San Francisco's Chris Brown is on his way.

None of them, however, is yet in Schmidt's class. The 36-year-old led the NL in homers (37) and RBIs (119) in '86. He also hit .290 and banged in 13 game-winning RBIs. Not bad for a guy who had been moved to first base to provide room for Rick Schu a year earlier. The return to third allowed manager John Felske the kind of flexibility he needed to rally the Phils to second place in the NL East last year. That's what a solid Mike Schmidt can do for you.

A veteran of knee surgery, Schmidt's range in the field may not be what it has been. But his glove remains solid, and his hitting is beyond question.

Shortstop
OZZIE SMITH
ST. LOUIS CARDINALS

An off-season vote of major-league managers taught us nothing we didn't know before. They decided, for example, that Ozzie Smith was the best shortstop in the National League. Surprise, surprise! They also voted Ozzie as the NL's smartest player. No shock there. The Cardinals' shortstop (since 1982) lost only one vote last year. That was for baseball gymnast of the year. The Cardinals no longer allow him to do his somersaults and backflips on the diamond. Too bad.

We've been picking the Wizard of Oz for this position as long as we can remember. We'll keep doing it as long as he can slip his glove onto his hand and walk onto the field. A half-speed Smith is better than anyone else in the business.

In a year when the Cardinals hit a pitiful .236 as a team (easily last in the NL), Ozzie enjoyed his best season with the stick (.280 and 54 RBIs). His defensive work is beyond belief. Only 5–10 and 150 pounds, he's extremely sturdy, getting into 153 games a year ago. Even at age 32, there is little chance that any other NL shortstop will overtake him for years to come.

The switch-hitting Redbird is surely headed to Cooperstown.

Outfield
TIM RAINES
MONTREAL EXPOS

Every general manager in the game cast his eyes toward Montreal as the '86 season drew to a close. Knowing that Tim Raines was set to become a free agent, the men who spend the bucks (and expect to win) knew that this man could help them.

Listen to Atlanta manager Chuck Tanner: "Raines is the best leadoff hitter — ever!" said the big-league veteran. "He's a great one!"

A one-time high school football star in Florida, Raines still relies on his great speed. That helped him win the NL batting title (.334) last year, along with a share of the on-base percentage lead (.413, with Keith Hernandez). He was also third in hits (194), third in triples (10), and third in stolen bases (70).

The 5–8, 180-pounder admits that he still has to work on his defense. "My arm isn't the best," he says. "But I'm getting better in the field. My speed really helps there, too." Raines is one of the best at charging balls in the outfield, cutting down on the distance he has to throw.

They call Raines "Rock." But the nickname has nothing to do with his defense. It's a salute to his body — hard, muscular, and quick. It'll help someone this season.

Outfield
TONY GWYNN
SAN DIEGO PADRES

Now that he has a glove to almost match his matchless bat, Tony Gwynn takes his place among baseball's top outfielders.

The hard-working Gwynn, the NL's No. 3 hitter in '86, has always swung a hot bat. He just missed his all-time high in hits (211 compared to 213 in 1984), while batting .329 (finishing behind Tim Raines and Steve Sax). He also banged 14 homers, nearly double his previous high.

But his new-found defense is even more pleasing to Gwynn. Ask the Cards' Willie McGee. One day last July, Gwynn flung his glove over the San Diego fence to rob the St. Louis speedball of a much-needed home run. "I'm doing all of it now," says Gwynn. "I'm hitting with more power, running well, playing defense. I'm getting there."

That's putting it mildly. He's there, friends. Tony has this nasty habit of down-playing his tremendous ability. National League pitchers would tell you that. Tony led the league in hitting in '84 with a sterling .351 mark, before finishing twice in the top four.

Obviously, he'll need some help in San Diego before he can lead the Padres back to the top. But Tony provides a great foundation upon which to build.

Outfield
DAVE PARKER
CINCINNATI REDS

We struggled mightily in making this pick. We weighed the chance of a major comeback by Dale Murphy of Atlanta, who had his worst season in five years last year, against the on-field performance of the Reds' hefty Dave Parker.

Parker, a Cincinnati native, has flourished since returning to his hometown. After some great years in Pittsburgh, it looked like Parker was finished. Then came the return to southern Ohio and a new life.

At age 35, Dave is still a fearsome slugger. Check his '86 stats. He smacked 31 homers (tied with Glenn Davis for second in the NL), knocked in 116 runs (second to Mike Schmidt's 119), and banged out 12 game-winning RBIs. He hit .273, with 174 hits (with 31 doubles), good numbers for a power man. His RBI total was 41 better than his teammate Buddy Bell, who was second on the Reds.

Though he may have lost a step or two, Parker's throwing arm more than makes up for it. And when he's running the bases, he scatters opponents as he lumbers along the base paths. We'll keep our eye on Murphy (who may or may not be the key to Atlanta's comeback hopes), but we'll put our money on Parker.

Catcher
GARY CARTER
NEW YORK METS

According to most National League fans, the Mets' catcher should be selling hot dogs. Some of them call him bush, the unkindest cut for a pro. But baseball folks call him great, and so do we.

At age 33, there are flaws in Carter's game. His foot speed is ordinary, and his arm is suspect. But there are few better catchers for directing a pitching staff. And he always seems to come up with the big hit when the Mets need it.

In a year when the world champ New Yorkers averaged .264 at the plate, the clean-up hitter hit only .255. But Carter still managed to lead the club in RBIs (105), with 24 homers. In fact, until a mid-August hand injury, he was leading the NL in RBIs.

In fairness, Gary often came to the plate with runners on base. The first three Met hitters — Len Dykstra, Wally Backman, and Keith Hernandez — each hit over .300. Still, it was the scrappy Californian who got the runs in.

"He's a player you dream about," says Gary's boss, Met manager Davey Johnson. "Forget the stat sheet. You just know he's helping you, both on offense and on defense." He's the key to the Mets' repeat chances.

Righthanded Pitcher
MIKE SCOTT
HOUSTON ASTROS

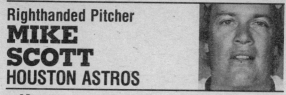

No one since King Kong has thrown such fear into the City of New York. In the 1933 movie of the same name, ape Kong terrorized the Big Apple. Astro righty Mike Scott did the same last fall. Everyone in New York knew the Mets would have to beat the Astros in Game 6 of the NL play-offs. Game 7 would have produced Scott, and the Mets' chances might have been shot.

No doubt that the ex-Met was the league's dominating pitcher down the stretch in '86. His split-fingered fastball was almost unhittable, whether or not he was scuffing the ball (as the Mets claimed). While his won-loss total of 18–10 wasn't overpowering, his ERA of 2.22 (the NL's best), his league-leading 306 strikeouts (in 275 innings), his leading total of five shutouts (plus another in the play-offs), and his flag-clinching no-hitter helped him win the NL 1986 Cy Young Award.

The split-fingered fastball saved Scott's career. As late as 1984, he went 5–11 with a 4.68 ERA. Ouch! No one could have blamed Mike if he looked into other job possibilities. But learning the new pitch (from current Giant manager Roger Craig) changed his style and his life. Scott went 18–8 in '85 before his 18–10 in '86.

Lefthanded Pitcher
FERNANDO VALENZUELA
LOS ANGELES DODGERS

Fans of Bobby Ojeda and other NL lefties may argue with us. But we'll go with the Dodgers' Fernando Valenzuela as our choice for the league's top southpaw for 1987. Ojeda (18–5 with a 2.57 ERA in '86) had a career year. Our man Fernando, however, has a super year every year, even with the Dodgers beginning to slip-slide away.

The chunky Mexican had his first 20-win season in '86, finishing at 21–11 with a 3.14 ERA. More important, he did it with a patched-up Dodger lineup; and he finished what he started 20 times during the season. That's eight more complete games than league runners-up Dwight Gooden and Rick Rhoden. In fact, Valenzuela has completed 43% of his career starts. (Mike Scott, on the other hand, has completed about 7% of his.)

Valenzuela does it with a combination of great speed plus a variety of outstanding pitches, including a mean screwball.

"Fernando never beats himself," says Houston's Phil Garner. "He pitches well, he can hit, and he's a surprisingly good fielder. He's one tough hombre."

The Dodgers' first 20-game winner in nine years, Fernando could use more support. But without it, he'll still win plenty.

Who will be baseball's next .400 hitter? The experts believe that Boston 3B Wade Boggs probably has the best chance.

American League TEAM PREVIEWS

AL East
TORONTO BLUE JAYS
1986 Finish: Fourth
1987 Prediction: First

Jesse Barfield

Tom Henke

Though the 1985 AL East champs slumped to fourth in '86, there's no reason to believe that they won't be in the hunt in '87. They have lots of firepower in their bats, a fine bullpen, and several true stars. All they need is more consistency from their starting pitchers and better play at third.

Manager Jimy Williams, beginning his second season, has great strength up the middle, with All-Pro SS Tony Fernandez (.310, 213 hits, 25 stolen bases, a great glove) and 2B Damaso Garcia (.281), whose shoulder woes kept him out of 40 games in '86. The outfield may be the AL's best, the Yanks and Red Sox included. All-Pro George Bell (.309, 31 homers, 108 RBIs) and rifle-armed Jesse Barfield (.289, a league-leading 40 homers, 108 RBIs) will do the job for years. CF Lloyd

Moseby (86 RBIs, 32 steals, 21 homers) completes the trio.

1B Willie Upshaw (.251, 23 steals) is okay, but changes may be made at 3B where Rance Mulliniks (.259) and Garth Iorg (.260) have split time for years. Young Kelly Gruber may get a shot, though his bat is suspect. C Ernie Whitt (.268) was an off-season free agent.

The bullpen is in super shape, with rookie star Mark Eichhorn (14–6, 10 saves, 1.72, 166 strikeouts) and Tom Henke (9–5, a club-record 27 saves). Free-agent P Jim Clancy was 14–14 but lost his last seven. One-time ace Dave Stieb flopped to 7–12 and must bounce back. Lefty Jimmy Key (14–11) ended '86 with 19⅔ consecutive scoreless innings. Righty Tom Filer (7–0 in '85, elbow surgery in '86) and rookie lefty Jeff Musselman could help. Mike Sharperson, up from Triple A, could replace Garcia at 2B.

STAT LEADERS — 1986

BATTING
Average: Fernandez, .310
Runs: Barfield, 107
Hits: Fernandez, 213
Doubles: Bell, 38
Triples: Fernandez, 9
Home Runs: Barfield, 40*
RBIs: Bell, Barfield, 108
Game-Winning RBIs: Bell, 15**
Stolen Bases: Moseby, 32

PITCHING
Wins: Eichhorn, Key, Clancy, 14
Losses: Clancy, 14
Complete games: Clancy, 6
Shutouts: Clancy, 3
Saves: Henke, 27
Walks: Stieb, 87
Strikeouts: Eichhorn, 166

*Led league.
**Tied for league lead.

NEW YORK YANKEES
1986 Finish: Second
1987 Prediction: Second

Mike Pagliarulo

Dave Righetti

George "Boss" Steinbrenner made the first good move of the off-season when he signed manager Lou Piniella for another two years. In George's way, that means Lou will open spring training. How much longer he lasts may depend on the first few games.

With one-time Yank SS Bucky Dent waiting in the Yanks' minor-league wings, Piniella will have to get some arms to do better in '87. If those arms are attached to top-notch starting pitchers, Lou could win it all (and survive for another year). The '86 Yanks hit a ton, but lost too many 10–9 and 9–8 games. Of course, the best arm belongs to LP Dave Righetti (8–8), whose 46 saves set a major-league record. He clicked on 24 straight save opportunities. Ex-Pirate Rick Rhoden (15–12) should be a big help.

Otherwise, Lou will turn to young Yank hurlers Bob Tewksbury (9–5) and Scott Nielsen (4–4). Dennis Rasmussen (18–6), '86's most pleasant surprise, is back; and Ron "Gator" Guidry (9–12) could bounce back.

The offense is positively explosive. 1B Don Mattingly (.352, an all-time Yank record 238 hits, 53 league-leading doubles, 31 homers, 113 RBIs, .573 slugging percentage) may be the best player in the game — anywhere. 2B Willie Randolph (.276) remains a pro, but his SS partner (will Wayne Tolleson be the guy?) is a problem. 3B Mike Pagliarulo (.238, 28 homers) slumped late.

Despite his long feud with Boss George, RF Dave Winfield (.262, 104 RBIs) is still among the AL's best. So is CF Rickey Henderson (.263 and 87 steals, tops in the league). There's lots of firepower, though the shortstop and catching spots could use some help. There's little on the farm.

STAT LEADERS — 1986

BATTING

Average: Mattingly, .352
Runs: Henderson, 130*
Hits: Mattingly, 238*
Doubles: Mattingly, 53*
Triples: Three with 5
Home Runs: Mattingly, 31
RBIs: Mattingly, 113
Game-Winning RBIs: Mattingly, 15**
Stolen Bases: Henderson, 87*

PITCHING

Wins: Rasmussen, 18
Losses: Guidry, 12
Complete Games: Guidry, 5
Shutouts: Nielsen, 2
Saves: Righetti, 46*
Walks: Rasmussen, 74
Strikeouts: Guidry, 140

*Led league.
**Tied for league lead.

AL East
BOSTON RED SOX
1986 Finish: First
1987 Prediction: Third

Dwight Evans

Marty Barrett

Post-World Series joke in New York: Bill Buckner was in town the other day. He tried to catch a cab. It went through his legs.

Those are the jokes that winners, even lucky ones, tell. Twice within a strike of the 1986 world title, the Sox blew it in seven tough games. History says that Boston wins the AL title once every decade. History will repeat. Sorry, John McNamara.

The Bosox won't go without a fight, however. There's plenty of sock in their bats. 3B Wade Boggs, the AL's best, will hit at least .330 again, which sets up a lot of scoring opportunities. (He was on base 45.3% of the time in '86.) He gets plenty of offensive help from All-Pro LF Jim Rice (.324, fifth in the AL, 110 RBIs, 20 homers) and near-All-Pro RF Dwight Evans (26 homers, 97 RBIs).

A fully healed Bill Buckner (.267, 102 RBIs) and postseason hero Marty Barrett (.286) offer plenty of strength on the right side of the infield. C Rich Gedman, who looked bad against Met lefties in the Series, hit .258 with 65 RBIs in '86 and is the AL's best. Ex-Mariner Dave Henderson, who rescued the Sox in Game 5 of the AL play-offs, should be the full-time CF.

Starting pitching starts with Cy Young and MVP Award winner Roger Clemens (24–4, 2.48, 238 strikeouts), the AL's top righty, and Bruce Hurst (13–8, 2.99). Oil Can Boyd (16–10) is outstanding, when his head is on straight. Despite his World Series failure, Calvin Schiraldi (4–2, 1.41) is a fine bull-pen closer. Middle relief, as the Mets proved, is a major problem. Wes Gardner may be the answer. Righty Rob Woodward could help, along with 1B Pat Dodson, C John Marzano, and OFs LaShelle Tarver and Ellis Burks.

STAT LEADERS — 1986

BATTING
Average: Boggs, .357*
Runs: Boggs, 107
Hits: Boggs, 207
Doubles: Boggs, 47
Triples: Owen, 7
Home Runs: Baylor, 31
RBIs: Rice, 110
Game-Winning RBIs: Baylor, 13
Stolen Bases: Barrett, 15

PITCHING
Wins: Clemens, 24*
Losses: Nipper, 12
Complete Games:
   Hurst, 11
Shutouts: Hurst, 4
Saves: Stanley, 16
Walks: Clemens, 67
Strikeouts: Clemens, 238

*Led league.

AL East
CLEVELAND INDIANS
1986 Finish: Fifth
1987 Prediction: Fourth

Cory Snyder   **Joe Carter**

In Cleveland, where many fans usually come disguised as empty seats, there's excitement brewing. The offense is in great shape, the starting pitching is coming, and the talent is arriving from the minors.

The Tribe may be just a few players away: a starting pitcher, a solid catcher, a sound reliever. Not bad.

Start with the double-play combo of All-Pro 2B Tony Bernazard (.301). and near-All-Pro SS Julio Franco (.306). 1B Pat Tabler (.326) and 3B Brook Jacoby (.288) complete a wonderful infield. They were the keys to Cleveland's team average of .284, by far the majors' best. If DH Andre Thornton (.229, 66 RBIs) bounces back from knee surgery, this group will be even better.

The outfield is powerful. Check Joe Carter's numbers: .302, 29 homers, and a league-leading 121 RBIs. He's a future superstar. Mel Hall (.296, 77 RBIs) isn't too shabby, either. And Cory Snyder (.272 as a rookie, with 24 homers) has great potential. Manager Pat Corrales sleeps well. One question: Can CF Brett Butler (.278, only 51 RBIs) bounce back from a so-so season?

The pitching is not quite as strong. The team's 4.58 ERA ranked 12th in the AL. Ken Schrom (14–7), Tom Candiotti (16–12), and hard-throwing lefty Greg Swindell (5–2, including four wins in a row in September) will probably join ancient Phil Niekro (11–11) as starters. The bullpen, led by Ernie Camacho (20 saves), needs help.

Among the newcomers, righty Jose Roman may find a spot, along with OFs Winston Ficklin, Dave Clark, and Rod Allen; catcher Kevin Buckley; and DH hopeful Bernardo Brito. Bright days are ahead.

STAT LEADERS — 1986

BATTING
Average: Tabler, .326
Runs: Carter, 108
Hits: Carter, 200
Doubles: Carter, 36
Triples: Butler, 14*
Home Runs: Carter, 29
RBIs: Carter, 121*
Game-Winning RBIs: Carter, Bernazard, 11
Stolen Bases: Butler, 32

PITCHING
Wins: Candiotti, 16
Losses: Candiotti, 12
Complete Games: Candiotti, 17*
Shutouts: Candiotti, 3
Saves: Camacho, 20
Walks: Candiotti, 106
Strikeouts: Candiotti, 167

*Led league.

AL East
DETROIT TIGERS
1986 Finish: Third
1987 Prediction: Fifth

Walt Terrell   **Lou Whitaker**

Except for a brief run following the All-Star break, the 1986 Tigers had, at best, an ordinary year. Without some major pitching improvement, it could happen again.

The Tigers' top off-season task was re-signing free-agent RHP Jack Morris, one of only three AL 20-game winners. Morris also led the league in shutouts (6), and finished third in complete games (15) and strikeouts (223). Walt Terrell (15–12) wasn't bad, and rookie Eric King (11–4) was brilliant, at times. But the starters, outside of Morris, were just fair. Willie Hernandez remains the king of the bullpen (8–7, 24 saves) with decent set-up work from Randy O'Neal.

There are lots of questions over the rest of the Tiger Stadium lawn. Will CF Chet Lemon (.251) bounce back from an off year?

Will 3B Darnell Coles (.273) continue to improve at third? Will C Lance Parrish, long the AL's best, recover from the back problems that kept him out of the lineup over the last two months of the season?

Much-traveled LF Dave Collins has traveled again, this time to Montreal. Free-agent Larry Herndon (.247) or American Association hitting champ Bruce Fields could take over. Kirk Gibson (.268, 26 homers, 86 RBIs, 34 steals) is one of the best.

If Parrish doesn't bounce back, watch for youngster Dwight Lowry (.307 in 50 games) or free-agent Mike Heath to take over. The infield, in addition to Coles, is fine, thank you. 1B Darrell Evans (29 homers, 85 RBIs), 2B Lou Whitaker (.269), and SS Alan Trammell (.277, 21 homers, 25 steals) will suit manager Sparky Anderson's needs. Ps Jack Lazorko and John Pacella, plus IFs German Rivera and Scott Madison might make a difference.

STAT LEADERS — 1986

BATTING
Average: Trammell, .277
Runs: Trammell, 107
Hits: Trammell, 159
Doubles: Trammell, 33
Triples: Trammell, 7
Home Runs: Evans, 29
RBIs: Coles, Gibson, 86
Game-Winning RBIs: Gibson, 12
Stolen Bases: Gibson, 34

PITCHING
Wins: Morris, 21
Losses: Terrell, 12
Complete Games:
   Morris, 15
Shutouts: Morris, 6*
Saves: Hernandez, 24
Walks: Terrell, 98
Strikeouts: Morris, 223

*Led league.

AL East
BALTIMORE ORIOLES
1986 Finish: Seventh
1987 Prediction: Sixth

Cal Ripken, Jr.   **Don Aase**

The Orioles finished the '86 season in an unfamiliar pose: at the bottom of the AL East. It probably won't happen again.

Old hand Cal Ripken, Sr., replaces twice-manager Earl Weaver. One of his first major decisions: where to play Cal Ripken, Jr.? Long the AL's top shortstop, Junior may be headed to 3B, taking his glove, his range, his .282 average, and his consecutive-games streak with him. Stay tuned.

While Ripken never misses an inning, injuries have robbed his powermates, 1B Eddie Murray and CF Fred Lynn. Murray led the O's in batting (.305) and RBIs (84) last year, despite nearly a month on the disabled list. Lynn (.287) missed one third of the season and is rapidly developing a "doesn't-play-hurt" rap. The trio had RBIs in the same game only three times last year.

The major Baltimore addition is ex-Padre Terry Kennedy (.264), the professional catcher GM Hank Peters was seeking. He'll catch a rebuilding pitching staff.

Storm Davis left in the Kennedy trade. Scott McGregor (11–15, 4.52); Mike Flanagan, an off-season free agent (7–11, 4.24); and Mike Boddicker (14–12, but 4.70) will have to improve. Look for John Habyan, a fine righty, to join the rotation, along with lefty Eric Bell.

The bullpen starts with ace righthanded closer Don Aase (6–7, but 34 important saves). The Orioles' pen earned only 39 saves all year.

Chris Padget will get a long look at 1B (Murray would DH) as will OF Ken Gerhart, who had a good trial last September.

There's lots for Ripken and Peters to do. They'll have to improve the pitching *and* the defense. But it can be done.

STAT LEADERS — 1986

BATTING
Average: Murray, .305
Runs: Ripken, 98
Hits: Ripken, 177
Doubles: Ripken, 35
Triples: Shelby, 4
Home Runs: Ripken, 25
RBIs: Murray, 84
Game-Winning RBIs: Ripken, 15*
Stolen Bases: Wiggins, 21

PITCHING
Wins: Boddicker, 14
Losses: McGregor, 15
Complete Games:
   Boddicker, 7
Shutouts: McGregor, 2
Saves: Aase, 34
Walks: Dixon, 83
Strikeouts: Boddicker, 175

*Tied for league lead.

AL East
MILWAUKEE BREWERS
1986 Finish: Sixth
1987 Prediction: Seventh

Robin Yount

Paul Molitor

New manager Tom Trebelhorn has some pluses and some minuses in his Milwaukee dugout as he begins his first full season as the Brewers' field boss.

There's All-Pro lefty Teddy Higuera (20–11, 2.79, 15 complete games, four shutouts), who can anchor any pitching staff. Robin Yount and Paul Molitor are a couple of outstanding veterans. Yount, one of the game's youngest old-timers, has 13 big-league years behind him at age 31. Robin was sixth among AL batters (.312), and did his usual all-around professional job. Molitor, a nine-year vet, weighed in at .281, with 55 RBIs and 20 steals. And there are some fine youngsters, like OF Rob Deer (.232), who cracked 33 homers (fourth in the AL) but struck out 179 times. A mixed bag. 2B Dale

Sveum (.246) enjoyed a 14-game hitting streak, and P Juan Nieves went 11–12, but struggled late in the year.

The Brewers' catching staff will be totally revamped. Gone are Charlie Moore and Rick Cerone. In are former first-round draftee B.J. Surhoff (.308 at Triple A), Charlie O'Brien (.324 at Double A), and Bill Schroeder (off the disabled list).

Trebelhorn will look for improvement from former All-Pro Cecil Cooper (.258) and SS Ernest Riles (.252). He'll probably start the year without other veteran Brewers, like Ben Oglivie and Gorman Thomas. But ex-Dodger Greg Brock (16 homers) will be on hand.

Though the starting pitching is shaky, the bullpen is decent, with Mark Clear (5–5, 2.20, 16 saves) and young Dan Plesac (10–7, 14 saves). There's plenty of help on the farm, including OFs Mike Felder, Jim Adduci, and Alan Cartwright; SS Edgar Diaz; P Don August; and 1B Joey Meyer. The Brewers are a couple of years away.

STAT LEADERS — 1986

BATTING
Average: Yount, .312
Runs: Yount, 82
Hits: Yount, 163
Doubles: Yount, 31
Triples: Yount, 6
Home Runs: Deer, 33
RBIs: Deer, 86
Game-Winning RBIs: Riles, 12
Stolen Bases: Molitor, 20

PITCHING
Wins: Higuera, 20
Losses: Three with 12
Complete Games:
    Higuera, 15
Shutouts: Higuera, 4
Saves: Clear, 16
Walks: Nieves, 77
Strikeouts: Higuera, 207

AL West
TEXAS RANGERS
1986 Finish: Second
1987 Prediction: First

Pete Incaviglia   **Pete O'Brien**

If young manager Bobby Valentine can
hold his mostly young pitching staff together
from now until October, there could be big
doings in Texas. Knuckleballing Charlie
Hough (17–10) is the old man of the staff, at
age 38. But the youngsters lack only experience, not ability. Bobby Witt (11–9, but 5.48)
and Ed Correa (12–14, 4.23), last year's
righthanded rookie sensations, became the
first pair of AL rookies to fan 150 or more
opponents in a season. Witt fanned 174;
Correa, 189. In addition, Witt won his last
seven decisions in 1986. The relief staff is
in great shape, with Greg Harris (10–8, 20
saves) and '86 rookies Dale Majorcic (2–4,
2.51) and Matt Williams (8–6, 3.58, in 80
appearances).

There are plenty of runs in the Ranger

bats. 1B Pete O'Brien (.290) swatted 23 homers and knocked in 90 runs. In the outfield, LF Gary Ward (.316), a free agent, is probably gone, but CF Oddibe McDowell (.266, 18 homers, 33 steals) and RF rookie Ruben Sierra (.264, 16 homers) will be back. Leading DH Larry Parrish (.276) provides lots of power (28 homers, 94 RBIs). C Don Slaught (.264) does a fine job. Young Pete Incaviglia, despite an all-time strikeout record, slugged 30 homers (tying the Ranger mark), including nine in September.

Valentine is optimistic about the coming season. He expects even more from Incaviglia, whose '86 play pleased him greatly. Texas is building from within, like most great clubs. Look for OFs Bob Brower and Javier Ortiz, 2B Jerry Browne and Jose Mota, 3B Jeff Moronko, and Ps Kevin Brown and Scott Anderson to get long early looks. Valentine could have this club near the top for years.

STAT LEADERS — 1986

BATTING
Average: Ward, .316
Runs: McDowell, 105
Hits: O'Brien, 160
Doubles: Fletcher, 34
Triples: Sierra, 10
Home Runs: Incaviglia, 30
RBIs: Parrish, 94
Game-Winning RBIs: O'Brien, 14
Stolen Bases: McDowell, 33

PITCHING
Wins: Hough, 17
Losses: Guzman, 15
Complete Games:
   Hough, 7
Shutouts: Hough,
   Correa, 2
Saves: Harris, 20
Walks: Witt, 143*
Strikeouts: Correa, 189

*Led league.

AL West
OAKLAND ATHLETICS
1986 Finish: Third (tied)
1987 Prediction: Second

Joaquin Andujar   **Carney Lansford**

If the Athletics' (not just A's anymore) pitchers spend more time with the pitching coach than the team doctor, Tony LaRussa might really enjoy his first full year as the Oakland manager.

The bullpen is a major problem. The lack of a good lefty closer (not to mention a top setup man) cost ex-Card Joaquin Andujar (12–7, 3.82) at least a couple of wins. Both Andujar and veteran righty Moose Haas (7–2, 2.74 in only 12 games) spent time with the doctor last year. Lefty Curt Young (13–9, 3.45) was the staff's top winner, though DH Dave Kingman, who stroked 12 of his 35 homers when Young was on the mound, may be gone. Jay Howell (3–6, 16 saves) should hang on in the bullpen while LaRussa tries to find help.

There's plenty of power in the Oakland bats. LF Jose Canseco (.240, 29 doubles, 33 homers, 117 RBIs — including 14 game-winners) lived up to his preseason billing, becoming the AL's '86 Rookie of the Year. Oakland re-signed free-agent CF Dwayne Murphy (.252), who missed nearly half the season with surgery for a spinal disc injury. SS Alfredo Griffin was the team's top everyday hitter (.285), and he's sturdy (335 straight games played). 1B Carney Lansford (.284) reached a personal high in homers (19). 2B Tony Phillips (.256) is recovered from a knee injury. Among the youngsters, C Terry Steinbach (.333 the last week of the season) should get a shot.

There will be some room for other young players. Most experts don't see the team retaining Dusty Baker or Wayne Gross. OFs Stan Javier and Luis Polonia; IFs Mark McGwire, Rob Nelson, and Jose Tolentino; and Ps Joey McLaughlin and Todd Burns will also be watched.

STAT LEADERS — 1986

BATTING
Average: Griffin, .285
Runs: Canseco, 85
Hits: Griffin, 169
Doubles: Canseco, 29
Triples: Griffin, 6
Home Runs: Kingman, 35
RBIs: Canseco, 117
Game-Winning RBIs: Canseco, 14
Stolen Bases: Griffin, 33

PITCHING
Wins: Young, 13
Losses: Rijo, 11
Complete Games:
    Andujar, 7
Shutouts: Young, 2
Saves: Howell, 16
Walks: Rijo, 108
Strikeouts: Rijo, 176

AL West
KANSAS CITY ROYALS
1986 Finish: Third (tied)
1987 Prediction: Third

Frank White   **George Brett**

The return of manager Dick Howser, hopefully recovered from brain-tumor surgery, should lift the Royals. More solid hitting and more runs would certainly increase the Royals' chances and improve Houser's health.

The Royals' top offensive man, 3B George Brett (.290, 17 homers, 73 RBIs in only 124 games) remains the key. Brett had surgery on his right (throwing) shoulder last November, but should be ready for a great '87. He still owns one of the game's most beautiful swings. Kaycee's .252 team batting average (tied for 12th in the AL) must rise. CF Willie Wilson hit only .269, but hit more homers (9) and knocked in more runs (44). C Jim Sundberg wound up at .212, after struggling under .200 much of the season.

His arm seems to be shot, too. SS Angel Salazar (.245) and Buddy Biancalana (.242) made 32 errors between them in '86. The DH combo of Jorge Orta (.277) and Hal McRae (.252) has had it. Howser's counting on 2B Frank White (.272) and 1B Steve Balboni (.229), who cracked 29 homers. A serious back problem may hamper slugger Balboni.

Pitching is a problem. The '85 Cy Young winner, Bret Saberhagen (7–12), never won two in a row in '86. Relief ace Dan Quisenberry (3–7) slumped to 12 saves, after never having fewer than 35 before. Steve Farr (8–4) is now the key to the bullpen. Charlie Leibrandt (14–11) hurled eight complete games, and Mark Gubicza (12–6) is still growing.

While the Royals wait for football star Bo Jackson to develop, young Kevin Seitzer (.323 in 27 late-season games) might be ready to step in. Bill Pecota should get a shot, with Greg Pryor gone. Ex-Mariner Danny Tartabull (96 RBIs) will be an instant hit in KC.

STAT LEADERS — 1986

BATTING
Average: Brett, .290
Runs: Smith, 80
Hits: Wilson, 170
Doubles: White, 37
Triples: Wilson, 7
Home Runs: Balboni, 29
RBIs: Balboni, 88
Game-Winning RBIs: White, 11
Stolen Bases: Wilson, 34

PITCHING
Wins: Leibrandt, 14
Losses: Leonard, 13
Complete Games:
    Leibrandt, 8
Shutouts: Three with 2
Saves: Quisenberry, 12
Walks: Gubicza, 84
Strikeouts: Gubicza, 118

AL West
MINNESOTA TWINS
1986 Finish: Sixth
1987 Prediction: Fourth

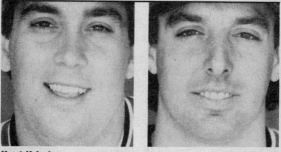

Kent Hrbek   **Gary Gaetti**

Plenty of new faces should populate the Minneapolis Humphrey Homerdome as the Twins search for the pitching, defense, and speed that will return them to the top of the AL West. There's plenty of offense in Minny, but other problems have doomed them to the bottom rungs. It will present a real challenge for new manager Tom Kelly, a former Twins' coach.

Take 3B Gary Gaetti, for example. His 34 homers were the most by a Twin since the great Harmon Killebrew cracked 41. But Gaetti's power and .287 average could bring a pitching arm or two in trade. CF Kirby Puckett, the chunky All-Pro star, swatted the ball at a .328 clip, with 31 homers, 96 RBIs, and 223 hits. He's untouchable. 1B Kent Hrbek, a hometown hero, still does the job

(.267, 29 homers, 91 RBIs). And RF Tom Brunansky (.256) provides plenty of offensive power. OF Randy Bush (.269) should return as a DH, with Billy Beane, the LF, recovered from bone-chip problems in his ankle.

None of the Twin catchers hit better than .244 last year, so look for a change in this department. Top winner, RHP Bert Blyleven (17–14) gave up an all-time record 49 homers last year. All told, the Twins' team ERA of 4.77 was easily the majors' worst. RHP Mike Smithson (16–13) should improve, with rookies like Les Straker, Ben Bianchi, Joe Klink, and Kevin Trudeau ready to step into the staff.

Mark Davidson and Phil Wilson may be ready to join the outfield. Hard-hitting Gene Larkin could become the DH in '87. Still, the big needs — a top catcher, a bullpen stopper, a fast outfielder — won't be solved easily. Look for more long days and nights in Minneapolis.

STAT LEADERS — 1986

BATTING
Average: Puckett, .328
Runs: Puckett, 119
Hits: Puckett, 223
Doubles: Puckett, 37
Triples: Bush, 7
Home Runs: Gaetti, 34
RBIs: Gaetti, 108
Game-Winning RBIs: Gaetti, 12
Stolen Bases: Puckett, 20

PITCHING
Wins: Blyleven, 17
Losses: Heaton, 15
Complete Games:
   Blyleven, 16
Shutouts: Blyleven, 3
Saves: Atherton, 10
Walks: Viola, 83
Strikeouts: Blyleven, 215

AL West
CALIFORNIA ANGELS
1986 Finish: First
1987 Prediction: Fifth

Wally Joyner   **Mike Witt**

The 1986 AL West champs (we picked 'em, few others did) came within one out of the league title and World Series. But their luck ran out, and manager Gene Mauch's quarter-century World Series drought continued. It will continue a while longer. The Angels are not likely to repeat.

1B Wally Joyner (.290, 22 homers, 100 RBIs in his rookie year) has a brilliant future. But many of his teammates are closer to Social Security checks than World Series checks. 3B Doug DeCinces (he's 36) can still do it (.256, 26 homers, 96 RBIs), and SS Dick Schofield (.249) has come a long way. The '86 club set a team record for fewest errors.

The Angels hope to re-sign LF Brian Downing (.267, 95 RBIs). Gary Pettis (.258) is a defensive whiz in center. RF is a potential problem area. At age 39, C Bob Boone will soon become the No. 1 catcher ever in games played. His defense is top-flight, though his bat is shot.

Mauch can rely on starters Mike Witt (18–10, 2.84) and Kirk McCaskill (17–10, 3.36). John Candelaria (10–2, 2.55, in 16 starts) must stay healthy, after an '86 bout with tendinitis. Don Sutton (15–11) will be 42 by opening day, which could be a problem. Still, it's the kind of staff a manager can rely on.

If his shoulder is sound, Donnie Moore (4–5, 21 saves) is a fine bullpen closer. Backup Doug Corbett (10 saves) is probably gone. Urbano Lugo, who has had previous trials, could make the staff. At age 22, 2B Mark McLemore may be ready to take over. Gus Polidor and Craig Gerber also have shots at infield spots.

If Pettis hits a little more and some quicker players develop, the Angels could challenge again.

STAT LEADERS — 1986

BATTING
Average: Joyner, .290
Runs: Pettis, 93
Hits: Joyner, 172
Doubles: Joyner, Downing, 27
Triples: Schofield, 6
Home Runs: DeCinces, 26
RBIs: Joyner, 100
Game-Winning RBIs: Joyner, 14
Stolen Bases: Pettis, 50

PITCHING
Wins: Witt, 18
Losses: Sutton, 11
Complete Games: Witt, 14
Shutouts: Witt, 3
Saves: Moore, 21
Walks: McCaskill, 92
Strikeouts: Witt, 208

CHICAGO WHITE SOX
1986 Finish: Fifth
1987 Prediction: Sixth

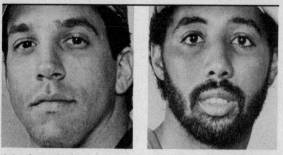

John Cangelosi   **Harold Baines**

With so many off-the-field problems swirling around them, it's little wonder that the Chisox have sunk so low into the AL West. There was the Ken Harrelson situation, which ended when Hawk quit last fall. And there was the ball-park situation — where will the team play in the future? Problem is, the Sox haven't come together as a team. There's some talent, but the players don't play well as a unit.

Despite a right knee that required post-season surgery, OF Harold Baines (.296, 21 homers, 88 RBIs) remains one of the AL's best. C-DH Ron Hassey (.323) also had knee surgery, after arriving from the Yankees as damaged goods. The outfield experiment ended(?), but C Carlton Fisk (.221) suffered with a sprained thumb. Where Fisk will play in '87 is still a question, but DH is the likeliest possibility. 1B Greg Walker (.277, 13 homers, 51 RBIs in 78 games) is first-rate. SS Ozzie Guillen (.250) can still rise to the top group of AL shortstops. And OF John Cangelosi (.235) impressed in his rookie year with 50 stolen bases.

Manager Jim Fregosi, who replaced Tony LaRussa at midseason last year, has his work cut out. The Sox simply did not execute on the field too often in '86. The bullpen is in decent shape. Rookie Bobby Thigpen had six saves and a win in eight appearances, then blew three straight. Dave Schmidt (8 saves) and Bob James (5–4, 14 saves) are solid. James and Neil Allen (7–2) came off the disabled list the last week of the '86 season and did well. If ex-Pirate Jose DeLeon (4–5, 2.96) can find his game, the Sox will benefit. Young owners of famous names, OF Mike Yastrzemski and P Bruce Tanner, could help, as could SS Tim Krauss.

STAT LEADERS — 1986

BATTING

Average: Baines, .296
Runs: Baines, 72
Hits: Baines, 169
Doubles: Baines, 29
Triples: Walker, 6
Home Runs: Baines, 21
RBIs: Baines, 88
Game-Winning RBIs: Baines, 10
Stolen Bases: Cangelosi, 50

PITCHING

Wins: Cowley, 11
Losses: Dotson, 17*
Complete Games:
   Bannister, 6
Shutouts: Allen, 2
Saves: James, 14
Walks: Cowley, 83
Strikeouts: Cowley, 132

*Tied for league lead.

AL West
SEATTLE MARINERS
1986 Finish: Seventh
1987 Prediction: Seventh

Mike Moore   **Phil Bradley**

Like so many other AL teams, the M's have a decent amount of hitting . . . and little else.

Fortunately, there are some young pitching prospects who might help Williams. Lefty Mark Langston (12–14, the team's top winner) showed a marked improvement in control in '86, walking 123 while striking out a league-high 245. Righties Mike Moore and Mike Morgan won 11 apiece and struck out 146 (Moore) and 116 (Morgan). Another righty, Mike Trujillo, tossed a one-hitter, only the second ever by a Mariner pitcher. Ex-Royals Scott Bankhead and Steve Shields and ex-Dodger Dennis Powell should help the mound crew, which will miss Matt Young (to LA).

While Langston led the league in strikeouts, so did the Mariner offense. They whiffed 1,148 times during the season, an AL record. Included were 20 K's suffered at the hands of Roger Clemens one fine spring day. Amazingly, C Scott Bradley was the AL's hardest-to-strike-out hitter. He hit .300 in 77 games. OF Phil Bradley finished with his third straight .300 season (.310, eighth in the league). OF Mike Kingery (Royals) and 2B Steve Watters (Dodgers) could help. Though the '86 M's set a team record for errors, 3B Jim Presley (.265, 107 RBIs) had a string of 43 errorless games. 1B Alvin Davis (.271, 18 homers) is rapidly becoming a Mariner all-timer. C Dave Valle, who hit .340 with five homers and 15 RBIs in 22 late-season games, may solve the team's catching problems. Ps Terry Taylor and Mike Campbell, SS Mario Diaz, and OFs Mickey Brantley and Dave Hangel may find work in Seattle.

STAT LEADERS — 1986

BATTING

Average: P. Bradley, .310
Runs: P. Bradley, 88
Hits: P. Bradley,
   Presley, 163
Doubles: Presley, 33
Triples: Tartabull, 6
Home Runs: Presley, 27
RBIs: Presley, 107
Game-Winning RBIs: Presley, 13
Stolen Bases: Reynolds, 30

PITCHING

Wins: Langston, 12
Losses: Morgan, 17**
Complete Games:
   Moore, 11
Shutouts: Three with 1
Saves: Young, 13
Walks: Langston, 123
Strikeouts: Langston, 245*

*Lead league.
**Tied for league lead.

A healthy SS Hubie Brooks is the key to the Expos' chances of overtaking Hubie's one-time teammates, the New York Mets.

National League TEAM PREVIEWS

NL East
NEW YORK METS
1986 Finish: First
1987 Prediction: First

Dwight Gooden   **Len Dykstra**

History is a great teacher. In major-league baseball, history teaches us that champions do not repeat. We flunk. We believe the Mets can — and will — do it again.

Why? Because the Mets have great talent in New York, great talent on the farm, and players who won without having career years (the best years of their careers).

Lefty P Bob Ojeda (18–5, 2.57) may have had his career year. But there's plenty of pitching depth, with RH Dwight Gooden (17–6, 2.84), RH Ron Darling (15–6, 2.81), RH Rick Aguilera (10–7), and Game 7 World Series hero LH Sid Fernandez (16–6). The twin bullpen closers, Jesse Orosco (8–6, 21 saves) and Roger McDowell (14–9, 22 saves), are awesome. The middle relief could be better, but not much.

Offensively, there's a ton of power with All-Pro C Gary Carter (.255, but a league-leading 16 game-winning RBIs, 105 RBIs overall, 24 homers) and RF Darryl Strawberry (.259, 27 homers, 93 RBIs). Lenny "Nails" Dykstra, whose homers keyed Mets' victories in the play-offs and Series, brings his .295 mark back to center field, and 1B Keith Hernandez (a consistent .310) owns the best first-base glove in the game. Series MVP Ray Knight (.298) is gone in a money squabble. But the rest of the crowd includes supers like Wally Backman; Mookie Wilson; and a deep, deep bench.

The Mets may have bought pennant insurance with ex-Padre slugger Kevin McReynolds (.287, 26 homers), but the price in young talent (Kevin Mitchell, Stan Jefferson, Shawn Abner) was steep. Still, the farm has 3B Dave Magadan, lefty Randy Meyers, SS Kevin Elster, and more. A dynasty? Not yet. But a repeat title could happen.

STAT LEADERS — 1986

BATTING
Average: Hernandez, .310
Runs: Hernandez, 94
Hits: Hernandez, 171
Doubles: Hernandez, 34
Triples: Dykstra, 7
Home Runs: Strawberry, 27
RBIs: Carter, 105
Game-Winning RBIs: Carter, 16*
Stolen Bases: Dykstra, 31

*Tied for league lead.

PITCHING
Wins: Ojeda, 18
Losses: McDowell, 9
Complete Games:
    Gooden, 12
Shutouts: Ojeda,
    Darling, Gooden, 2
Saves: McDowell, 22
Walks: Fernandez, 91
Strikeouts: Fernandez,
    Gooden, 200

NL East
PHILADELPHIA PHILLIES
1986 Finish: Second
1987 Prediction: Second

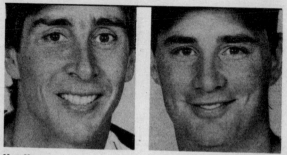

Von Hayes

Don Carman

The Phillies believe that the 1986 season started and finished too soon. The Phils struggled until the All-Star break, then started rolling. Not that anyone was beating the Mets in '86, of course. But the Phils thought they should have been closer.

Why not? Their offense is first-rate. MVP 3B Mike Schmidt, who says that '87 will be his last year, had a super season, with a league-leading 37 homers and 119 RBIs. That helped 1B Von Hayes (.305, 98 RBIs) to tie for the league lead in runs scored with 107. Only five Phils in history have combined a .300 season with 100+ runs scored. 2B Juan Samuel (.266, 78 RBIs, 42 stolen bases) makes a big contribution, along with RF Glenn Wilson (.271, 84 RBIs). If he's still a Phil, LF Gary Redus (.247) can hurt you. If

Redus is dealt, Greg Gross, Ron Roenicke, Jeff Stone, and Chris James (off ankle problems) could fill in. If Darren Daulton recovers from serious knee surgery, the catching could be in decent shape.

There's some fine young pitching, notably from a healthy Shane Rawley, Kevin Gross (12–12), lefty Bruce Ruffin (9–4, 2.46), and lefty Don Carman (10–5, 3.22). Carman's shoulder may be a problem, however, which may send him to the bullpen along with super closer Steve Bedrosian (8–6, 29 saves). Bedrosian had 16 saves in 22 September games.

The Phils, looking for another quality starter, may turn to Marvin Freeman (2–0 in three late-season games). If Daulton isn't healthy, the Phils also need a catcher. Meanwhile, rookies like James, OF Ron Jones, and 2B Greg Legg could play a role. Manager John Felske has a new contract.

STAT LEADERS — 1986

BATTING
Average: Hayes, .305
Runs: Hayes, 107**
Hits: Hayes, 186
Doubles: Hayes, 46**
Triples: Samuel, 12
Home Runs: Schmidt, 37*
RBIs: Schmidt, 119*
Game-Winning RBIs: Hayes, 14
Stolen Bases: Samuel, 42

PITCHING
Wins: Gross, 12
Losses: Gross, 12
Complete Games:
　Rawley, Gross, 7
Shutouts: Gross, 2
Saves: Bedrosian, 29
Walks: Gross, 94
Strikeouts: Gross, 154

*Led league.
**Tied for league lead.

NL East
ST. LOUIS CARDINALS
1986 Finish: Third
1987 Prediction: Third

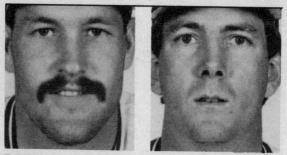

Todd Worrell   **John Tudor**

There are three kinds of lies: lies, awful
lies, and statistics. But it's no lie that one stat
sums up the '86 season for the Cards: batting average — .236. It was the offense that
brought the 1985 NL title to St. Louis. It was
lack of same that sank the Redbirds in '86.
It was the worst performance in the majors,
a full 11 points behind the No. 25 team, the
Chicago White Sox.

Manager Whitey Herzog knows that
there's no way that the Card gang can ever
duplicate that kind of disaster. First, he'll
have 1B Jack Clark back. St. Louis's pow-
erman was lost for the season last June 24
with torn thumb ligaments. As a result, St.
Loo hit only 58 homers all season. No other
team hit fewer than 110. A classic power
failure.

SS Ozzie Smith (.280) remains the game's top shortstop. His DP partner, Tommy Herr, hero of the '85 champs, should bounce back from his .252 season. RF Andy Van Slyke is one of the top fielders and throwers in the game. Vincent Coleman (.232, 107 steals) is the first player to ever steal 100 or more bases in each of his first two seasons. Still, Herzog needs a righthanded hitter in the lineup and a healthy Willie McGee, coming off serious knee surgery, warns that he'll take his time coming back.

Is Todd Worrell for real? The ace rookie reliever of '86 is counted on to repeat his numbers: a league-leading 36 saves, 2.08 ERA, LHPs John Tudor (13–7) and Greg Mathews (11–8) are the core of the mound staff, which will miss lefty Ken Dayley (elbow surgery) until at least June. Big (6–6) Joe Magrane, a lefty, may make the starting rotation after only a half season in Triple A. 1B Jim Lindeman could fit in, too.

STAT LEADERS — 1986

BATTING
Average: Smith, .280
Runs: Coleman, 94
Hits: Smith, 144
Doubles: Herr, 30
Triples: Coleman, 8
Home Runs: Van Slyke, 13
RBIs: Van Slyke, Herr, 61
Game-Winning RBIs: Herr, 12
Stolen Bases: Coleman, 107*

PITCHING
Wins: Forsch, 14
Losses, Cox, 13
Complete Games:
  Cox, 8
Shutouts: None
Saves: Worrell, 36*
Walks: Forsch, 68
Strikeouts: Cox, 108

*Led league.

NL East
CHICAGO CUBS
1986 Finish: Fifth
1987 Prediction: Fourth

Ryne Sandberg   **Lee Smith**

It's time to rebuild again in Chicago. That's dangerous talk, because the neighbors in Wrigleyville always think that means rebuilding Wrigley Field (with lights). We'll leave that discussion to others. Let's concentrate on the baseball team.

GM Dallas Green and his people are determined to get the older fellows out of Chicago. There's a solid foundation. The middle infielders are first-rate. Young SS Shawon Dunston, once the top pick in the baseball draft, has the best "gun" of any shortstop in the game. What an arm! His .250 bat mark with 68 RBIs should improve, but defensive lapses could force him to an outfield spot. His running mate, 2B Ryne Sandberg (.284, 34 steals) is a total professional. 1B Leon Durham (.262) remains a threat at the plate; and OF Keith Moreland, a poor outfielder, can still hurt you with his bat.

There's a big hole at 3B where vet Ron Cey (.273) has had it. There's no problem behind the plate where Jody Davis (.250) is one of the NL's best.

Manager Gene Michael believes that Chicago pitchers will have to learn to bust pitches inside to rival hitters. He may have a point. Pitching will be even better if Rick Sutcliffe and Dennis Eckersley (11 wins between them in '86) return to good health. Chicago's team ERA of 4.49 was easily the worst in the NL last year. Things could have been worse had not reliever Lee Smith (9–9, 31 saves) become the first pitcher ever with 30+ saves in three straight years.

The outfield could be helped with such Cub hopefuls as Steve Hammond, Brian Dayett, Chico Walker, Rafael Palmeiro, and Dave Martinez. Look for lefty Drew Hall to help the mound staff.

STAT LEADERS — 1986

BATTING
Average: Sandberg, .284
Runs: Moreland, 72
Hits: Sandberg, 178
Doubles: Dunston, 36
Triples: Durham, 7
Home Runs: Matthews, Davis, 21
RBIs: Moreland, 79
Game-Winning RBIs: Dunston, 8
Stolen Bases: Sandberg, 34

PITCHING
Wins: Smith, Sanderson, 9
Losses: Sutcliffe, 14
Complete Games:
    Sutcliffe, 4
Shutouts: Three with 1
Saves: Smith, 31
Walks: Sutcliffe, 96
Strikeouts: Eckersley, 137

NL East
MONTREAL EXPOS
1986 Finish: Fourth
1987 Prediction: Fifth

Floyd Youmans   **Hubie Brooks**

Montreal manager Buck Rodgers figures if he spends more time with lineup cards and less with hospital reports in '87, the Expos could mount a serious challenge in the NL East.

He's right, of course, provided free-agents Tim Raines and Andre Dawson are still around. LF Raines, the game's top leadoff hitter (tied for the league lead in on-base percentage at .413, a league-leading .334 batting average, 70 stolen bases, and improved defense), will "make" any club. RF Dawson (.284) remains a major threat.

The healthy return of SS Hubie Brooks (.340, 58 RBIs, 10 game-winners in only 80 games before his hand injury) is absolutely vital. CF Mitch Webster (.290, a league-leading 13 triples) is a solid pro, 3B Tim

Wallach (.233, 18 homers) was the subject of winter trade talks. If he goes, Jeff Reynolds (29 homers, 113 RBIs in Double A) could fill the gap.

Pitching is in fair shape. Young righty Floyd Youmans (13–12, 202 strikeouts), Dwight Gooden's high school teammate, is for real. So is Andy McGaffigan (10–5, 2.65). If LH Joe Hesketh recovers from elbow surgery, it will help. If not, look for Jay Tibbs, Dennis Martinez, late-season sensation Bob Sebra, and Rodger Cole to help. The bullpen is in good hands, led by big Jeff Reardon (7–9, 35 saves).

Just as frightening as the free-agent pictue is the Montreal attendance. It set an all-time Olympic Stadium low last season. Youngsters like C Wil Tejada, 1B Mike Hocutt, and OF Alonzo Powell will join returnees like P Bryn Smith (10–8) and 1B Andres Galarraga to lure Montrealers back into the Expo home.

STAT LEADERS — 1986

BATTING
Average: Raines, .334*
Runs: Raines, 91
Hits: Raines, 194
Doubles: Raines, 35
Triples: Webster, 13*
Home Runs: Dawson, 20
RBIs: Dawson, 78
Game-Winning RBIs: Brooks, 10
Stolen Bases: Raines, 70

PITCHING
Wins; Youmans, 13
Losses: Youmans, 12
Complete Games:
  Youmans, 6
Shutouts: Youmans,
  Tibbs, 2
Saves: Reardon, 35
Walks: Youmans, 118*
Strikeouts: Youmans, 202

*Led league.

NL East
PITTSBURGH PIRATES
1986 Finish: Sixth
1987 Prediction: Sixth

R.J. Reynolds   **Johnny Ray**

When you're in the pits, there are two
ways to build. You can turn to your farm
system for talented young people. Or you
can trade for proven talent. The Pirates' farm
system doesn't have much. And the problem with trades is that you usually have to
give up your better players — of which the
Pirates have few.

Every trade discussion centered around
C Tony Pena and P Rick Rhoden. Pena, one
of the most exciting catchers in the game,
raised his average from .241 to .288 from
mid-July to the end of the season. Righty
Rhoden (15–12) was sent to the Yanks for
youngsters Doug Drabek, Brian Fisher, and
Logan Easley, all right-handers.

There are other strengths, of course.
There's 2B Johnny Ray (.301, 78 RBIs) and 1B

Sid Bream, the former Dodger. Bream hit .270 with 16 homers, and set a National League record for assists by a first sacker. 3B Jim Morrison had a super '86, including a .274 average, 23 homers, and 88 RBIs. CF Barry Bonds, son of former star Bobby Bonds, is a solid addition (36 steals, 16 homers).

That, unfortunately, is about all for manager Jim Leyland to cheer about. The starting pitchers are just so-so, although Drabek may help. Don Robinson, now healthy, is the bullpen leader. He had 14 saves in '86. The Bucs will simply have to score more runs this season to make a difference. Pittsburgh played 53 one-run games a year ago — and lost 37 of them.

Watch for a trio of youngsters to get a shot at pitching slots. They include righties Stan Fansler and Jim Neidlinger, and lefty Bob Patterson. 3B Jeff King might fit in somewhere.

STAT LEADERS — 1986

BATTING
Average: Ray, .301
Runs: Bream, 73
Hits: Ray, 174
Doubles: Bream, 37
Triples: Orsulak, 6
Home Runs: Morrison, 23
RBIs: Morrison, 88
Game-Winning RBIs: Morrison, Bream, 9
Stolen Bases: Bonds, 36

PITCHING
Wins: Rhoden, 15
Losses: Reuschel, 16
Complete Games: Rhoden, 12
Shutouts: Reuschel, 2
Saves: Robinson, 14
Walks: Bielecki, 83
Strikeouts: Rhoden, 159

CINCINNATI REDS
1986 Finish: Second
1987 Prediction: First

Bill Gullickson
Eric Davis

The old gang is just about gone. Hail to the new gang. Tony Perez is now a coach. Pete Rose is now just a manager (at least until May 15 through some off-season roster moves). Dave Concepcion is nearing the end. Enter Eric Davis and Kal Daniels in the outfield (along with old-timer Dave Parker). Enter Barry Larkin at shortstop, possibly with Kurt Stillwell at second. Now if Rose's Reds can add a pitcher or two, it could be the start of something big.

Davis (.277, 27 homers, 80 stolen bases) has greatness written all over him. It won't be long before they start making comparisons with stars of the past. (We advise Davis to keep his ears shut.) Parker (.273, 31 homers, 116 RBIs) has at least a couple of All-Pro seasons ahead. The Reds are so deep in the outfield that youngsters like Tracy Jones and Paul O'Neill might well become first sackers, a position of need right now. Someone who can hit with power would be just what Dr. Rose ordered.

3B Nick Esasky could become trade bait as Cincy looks to shore up its pitching. The mound should provide opportunities for youngsters like righty Jeff Gray (up from Double A) and Rob Murphy (6–0, 0.72 in 34 appearances after the All-Star break). Ex-reliever Ted Power, a flop in the bullpen, starred as a starter (5–0 in September). With vet John Denny apparently gone, it will be up to Tom Browning (14–13) and Bill Gullickson (15–12) to firm up the staff, waiting to see if Mario Soto (5–10 in only 19 games) is healthy again. Lefty Chris Welsh (6–9) is a question mark, with Ron Robinson (10–3 and 14 saves) likely to remain in the bullpen. Righties Pat Pacillo and Bill Landrum could help, along with C Terry McGriff and 1B Lloyd McClendon.

STAT LEADERS — 1986

BATTING
Average: Bell, .278
Runs: Davis, 97
Hits: Parker, 179
Doubles: Parker, 31
Triples: Milner, 6
Home Runs: Parker, 31
RBIs: Parker, 116
Game-Winning RBIs: Parker, 12
Stolen Bases: Davis, 80

PITCHING
Wins: Gullickson, 15
Losses: Browning, 13
Complete Games:
  Gullickson, 6
Shutouts: Gullickson,
  Browning, 2
Saves: Franco, 29
Walks: Browning, 70
Strikeouts: Browning, 147

NL West
SAN FRANCISCO GIANTS
1986 Finish: Third
1987 Prediction: Second

Chili Davis   **Will Clark**

Were it not for some injuries that wiped out the Giants' power game and pitching staff, it could have been an even better summer of '86 in San Francisco. It wasn't bad, it says here, and it's getting better.

The Giants are building with solid young folks. That's obviously the way to go. A look around the infield must bring a smile to the face of manager (and pitching expert) Roger Craig. There's Will Clark (.287) at first, coming back from elbow surgery. There's rookie flash 2B Robby Thompson (.271), coming back from knee surgery. There's young SS Jose Uribe (.223 but a great glove) and exciting 3B Chris Brown (.317, before missing the last third of the season). In the outfield, Jeffrey Leonard (.279, 42 RBIs in only 89 games before a season-ending injury),

Chili Davis (.278, coming off shoulder surgery), and tough-guy Dan Gladden (.276). Bob Brenly (.246) is solid behind the plate.

Inspirational Mike Krukow (20–9, 3.05, 6–0 in September) is the Giants' first 20-game winner in 13 years. Lefty Mark Davis (5–7) adds a split-fingered fastball in '87. And righty Mike LaCoss (10–13) should bounce back to his early-season form of '86 (he was 9–3 at the All-Star break). Scott Garrelts (13–9) can start or relieve and do both well. That's rare.

The Giants are well stocked with pinch hitters, including the master, ex-Dodger Candy Maldonado (.252); Joel Youngblood; and Harry Spilman, who was an off-season free agent.

The Giant push produced the second-highest attendance mark in San Francisco history. The addition of a couple of solid pitchers, particularly a bullpen closer, could make it an even better season in '87. Fewer visits to the team doctor would help, too.

STAT LEADERS — 1986

BATTING
Average: Brown, .317
Runs: Thompson, 73
Hits: Thompson, 149
Doubles: Maldonado, 31
Triples: Many with 3
Home Runs: Maldonado, 18
RBIs: Maldonado, 85
Game-Winning RBIs: Maldonado, 14
Stolen Bases: Gladden, 27

PITCHING
Wins: Krukow, 20
Losses: LaCoss, 13
Complete Games:
  Krukow, 10
Shutouts: Krukow, 2
Saves: Garrelts, 10
Walks: Blue, 77
Strikeouts: Krukow, 178

NL West
HOUSTON ASTROS
1986 Finish: First
1987 Prediction: Third

Kevin Bass   **Bill Doran**

They say — whoever *they* are — that pitching is 80% of baseball. If that's true, then manager-of-the-year Hal Lanier may have the Astros 80% of the way toward repeating in the NL West. If you're into math, just keep in mind that the Mets (3.11) and the Astros (3.15), the two NL 1986 division champions, easily led the NL in pitching.

The Houston starters are unreal. (The Mets held only the bullpen edge.) Begin with All-Pro righty Mike Scott (18–10, 2.22, 306 strikeouts). Armed with his dangerous split-fingered fastball, he overpowered NL hitters over the last two months of last season and figures to continue in '87. Add lefty Bob Knepper (17–12, 3.14), who should have won Game 6 of the NL play-offs; still-murderous Nolan Ryan (12–8, 3.34, 194 strikeouts), if he's healthy; and young Jim Deshaies (12–5); and you have a powerful rotation. The bullpen, with Charlie Kerfeld (11–2, 2.59) setting up Dave Smith (4–7, but 33 saves), can win you a pennant.

The only thing the offense lacks is power. Despite Billy Hatcher's 14th-inning homer in Game 6 of the play-offs, the 'Stros' power game is 1B Glenn Davis (.265, 31 homers, 101 RBIs, and .493 slugging percentage) — and then wait for Davis to come up again. Hitting's a key need for Houston. Still, there's good offensive punch from 2B Bill Doran (.276), RF Kevin Bass (.311, 20 homers), platoon 3B Denny Walling (.312), and ageless LF Jose Cruz (.278). If free-agent C Alan Ashby (.257) isn't back, the Astros will be hurting. Rookie Robbie Wine, son of former major-leaguer Bobby, may not be ready yet. Houston may try to find spots for rookie outfielders Cameron Drew and Ty Gainey.

STAT LEADERS — 1986

BATTING

Average: Bass, .311
Runs: Doran, 92
Hits: Bass, 184
Doubles: Bass, 33
Triples: Bass, 5
Home Runs: Davis, 31
RBIs: Davis, 101
Game-Winning RBIs: Davis, 16**
Stolen Bases: Doran, 42

PITCHING

Wins: Scott, 18
Losses: Knepper, 12
Complete Games:
   Knepper, 8
Shutouts:
   Scott, Knepper, 5*
Saves: Smith, 33
Walks: Ryan, 82
Strikeouts: Scott, 306*

*Led league.
**Tied for league lead.

NL West
LOS ANGELES DODGERS
1986 Finish: Fifth
1987 Prediction: Fourth

Rick Honeycutt

Mike Scioscia

Dodger manager Tommy Lasorda bled Dodger blue all over the place in '86. Trouble was, too many of his players were bleeding the real thing, which tied the worst season for the Dodgers in LA.

Good health could produce an upturn in '87, particularly for Pedro Guerrero, Mike Marshall, and Steve Sax. When Guerrero went down with a severe knee injury last spring, the Dodger hopes went down with him. He played in only 31 games last year, many at part-strength. Marshall missed a third of the season. Sax, an All-Pro, had heel surgery after the season.

Actually, the Dodgers aren't in bad shape. They've got Sax (.332, second in the NL) at second, aging Bill "Doggy" Madlock (.280) at third, and Franklin Stubbs (.226) at first, with Greg Brock gone (Brewers). Mike Scioscia (.251) is one of the best defensive catchers in the NL. If they're healthy, Guerrero and Marshall should do well in the corners of the LA outfield. Injuries allowed Ralph Bryant and Jose Gonzalez to get a shot in the outfield a year ago, while Jeff Hamilton played some at third. The experience helps. C Gil Reyes could break in.

The mound staff starts with a trio of proven winners. All-Pro lefty Fernando Valenzuela (21–11, 20 complete games) is the best, and righties Orel Hershiser (14–14) and Bob Welch (7–13, 3.28) aren't bad.

It's the bullpen that is Lasorda's major concern. The Dodgers haven't had a big closer in years, and that's a problem. Ex-Mariner lefty Matt Young (8–6, 13 saves) could fill the bill. Ex-Brewers Tim Leary (12–12) and Stan Crews should help. Look for 1B Larry See (107 RBIs in Triple A) and versatile Jon Debus to get shots in '87.

STAT LEADERS — 1986

BATTING
Average: Sax, .332
Runs: Sax, 91
Hits: Sax, 210
Doubles: Sax, 43
Triples: Sax, 4
Home Runs: Stubbs, 23
RBIs: Madlock, 60
Game-Winning RBIs: Sax, 11
Stolen Bases: Duncan, 48

PITCHING
Wins: Valenzuela, 21*
Losses: Hershiser, 14
Complete Games:
    Valenzuela, 20*
Shutouts: Valenzuela,
    Welch, 3
Saves: Howell, 12
Walks: Hershiser, 86
Strikeouts: Valenzuela, 242

*Led league.

NL West
ATLANTA BRAVES
1986 Finish: Sixth
1987 Prediction: Fifth

Andres Thomas　　　　　　　**Gene Garber**

The name most talked about in Atlanta this winter was Dale Murphy. Why not? The Braves' center fielder, a one-time catcher, enjoyed another excellent season in '86 (.265, 29 homers), though not a real Murphy season. Still, he's the best they have. So why all the talk? First, there were the experts who advised the Braves to trade the gentle giant. He'd bring big talent, they reasoned; and the Braves haven't won with him. Get another center fielder, said other experts, and move Murphy to right.

Time will tell, of course, but until he's dealt away, Murphy remains the heart of the Braves. 1B Bob Horner, an off-season free agent, is another key to the Atlanta future. 2B Glenn Hubbard (.225) is in trouble following a horrible season. SS Andres

Thomas (.251) is the Braves' present and future shortstop. He looks marvelous. His presence makes Rafael Ramirez available.

There'll be some changes in the outfield, regardless of the Murphy question. With Omar Moreno gone, Albert Hall, Terry Harper, Darryl Motley, and possibly Billy Sample will battle for a starting spot. There'll be another battle behind the plate, where Ossie Virgil (.223) didn't do the job.

Pitching is in fair shape, with none of the starters really ideal. Righty Rick Mahler, the big winner with 14 wins, was also the big loser (18). The Braves would be advised to get Doyle Alexander and David Palmer back for another shot. They should also think about shoring up an awful bullpen. Bruce Sutter has had arm problems, and Gene Garber needs some support. Rookie Tommy Glavine should fit into the rotation.

A pitcher, a hitter, and some team speed would help tremendously.

STAT LEADERS — 1986

BATTING

Average: Horner, .273
Runs: Murphy, 89
Hits: Murphy, 163
Doubles: Thomas, 47
Triples: Murphy, 7
Home Runs: Murphy, 29
RBIs: Horner, 87
Game Winning RBIs: Murphy, 12
Stolen Bases: Ramirez, 19

PITCHING

Wins: Mahler, 14
Losses: Mahler, 18*
Complete Games: Mahler, 7
Shutouts: Mahler, Smith, 1
Saves: Garber, 24
Walks: Smith, 105
Strikeouts: Palmer, 170

*Led league.

NL West
SAN DIEGO PADRES
1986 Finish: Fourth
1987 Prediction: Sixth

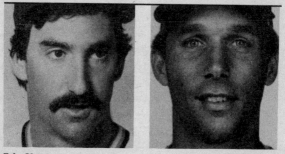

Eric Show　　　　　　　　　　　　**Tim Flannery**

For Larry Bowa, the joy didn't last long. Right after the former shortstop became the latest Padre manager, he learned that his top pitcher, Lamarr Hoyt, was in jail. Welcome to the big leagues, skipper.

Bowa takes over an old ball club that must be rebuilt with youth. The Padres, 1984 NL champs, sank badly in '86, with the old vets like Goose Gossage, Graig Nettles, and Steve Garvey failing to produce. Watch for a youth movement, possibly beginning with catcher Benito Santiago (veteran C Terry Kennedy was traded to Baltimore).

The outfield is solid. RF Tony Gwynn (.329, third in the NL) could become a regular finisher in the MVP race. LF John Kruk (.309) is a major-league hitter. CF Kevin McReynolds is gone, but the young Mets he brought should produce long-term gains.

SS Garry Templeton (.247) will have to increase his production. Watch for ex-Met Kevin Mitchell or Randy Asadoor (.364 in only 15 games) to get a full shot at the 3B job. 1B Tim Pyznarski could be ready to step in for Garvey.

If Hoyt isn't back, Bowa's pitching problems increase. Lefties Dave Dravecky and Craig Lefferts will join Eric Show in the rotation. Former Oriole Storm Davis, obtained for Kennedy, would help, unless he is traded again. Reliever Lance McCullers is the man to replace Gossage, and youngsters like lefties Ray Hayward and Ed Vosburg and righties Greg Booker and Jimmy Jones could win roster spots.

Replacing nice-guy Steve Boros could be a good thing for Bowa, provided he gets some timely hitting, more team speed, and consistent work from his starters.

STAT LEADERS — 1986

BATTING

Average: Gwynn, .329
Runs: Gwynn, 107
Hits: Gwynn, 211*
Doubles: Gwynn, 33
Triples: Gwynn, 7
Home Runs: McReynolds, 26
RBIs: McReynolds, 96
Game-Winning RBIs: McReynolds, 14
Stolen Bases: Gwynn, 37

*Led league.

PITCHING

Wins: McCullers, Hawkins, 10
Losses: Dravecky, Hoyt, 11
Complete Games: Dravecky, Hawkins, 3
Shutouts: Three with 1
Saves: Gossage, 21
Walks: Hawkins, 75
Strikeouts: Hawkins, 117

Though LA bombed in '86, the Dodgers know they can win anytime their lefty ace, Fernando Valenzuela, goes to the mound.

STATISTICS
1986

AMERICAN LEAGUE
Batting

(30 or more at-bats)
*Bats Lefthanded †Switch-Hitter

Batter and Club	AVG	G	AB	R	H	HR	RBI	SB
Allanson, Andy, Clev.	.225	101	293	30	66	1	29	10
Armas, Tony, Bos.	.264	121	425	40	112	11	58	0
Baines, Harold, Chi.*	.296	145	570	72	169	21	88	2
Baker, Dusty, Oak.	.240	83	242	25	58	4	19	0
Balboni, Steve, K.C.	.229	138	512	54	117	29	88	0
Bando, Chris, Clev.†	.268	92	254	28	68	2	26	0
Barfield, Jesse, Tor.	.289	158	589	107	170	40	108	8
Barrett, Marty, Bos.	.286	158	625	94	179	4	60	15
Bathe, Bill, Oak.	.184	39	103	9	19	5	11	0
Baylor, Don, Bos.	.238	160	585	93	139	31	94	3
Beane, Billy, Minn.	.213	80	183	20	39	3	15	2
Bell, George, Tor.	.309	159	641	101	198	31	108	7
Beniquez, Juan, Balt.	.300	113	343	48	103	6	36	2
Bergman, Dave, Det.*	.231	65	130	14	30	1	9	0
Bernazard, Tony, Clev.†	.301	146	562	88	169	17	73	17
Berra, Dale, N.Y.	.231	42	108	10	25	2	13	0
Biancalana, Buddy, K.C.†	.242	100	190	24	46	2	8	5
Bochte, Bruce, Oak.*	.256	125	407	57	104	6	43	3
Boggs, Wade, Bos.*	.357	149	580	107	207	8	71	0
Bonilla, Bobby, Chi.†	.269	75	234	27	63	2	26	4
Bonilla, Juan, Balt.	.243	102	284	33	69	1	18	0
Bonnell, Barry, Sea.	.196	17	51	4	10	0	4	0
Boone, Bob, Cal.	.222	144	442	48	98	7	49	1
Boston, Daryl, Chi.*	.266	56	199	29	53	5	22	9
Bradley, Phil, Sea.	.310	143	526	88	163	12	50	21
Bradley, Scott, Chi.-Sea.*	.300	77	220	20	66	5	28	1
Braggs, Glenn, Milw.	.237	58	215	19	51	4	18	1
Brantley, Mickey, Sea.	.196	27	102	12	20	3	7	1
Brett, George, K.C.*	.290	124	441	70	128	16	73	1
Brookens, Tom, Det.	.270	98	281	42	76	3	25	11
Brunansky, Tom, Minn.	.256	157	593	69	152	23	75	12

Batter and Club	AVG	G	AB	R	H	HR	RBI	SB
Buckner, Bill, Bos.*	.267	153	629	73	168	18	102	6
Buechele, Steve, Tex.	.243	153	461	54	112	18	54	5
Burleson, Rick, Cal.	.284	93	271	35	77	5	29	1
Bush, Randy, Minn.*	.269	130	357	50	96	7	45	5
Butler, Brett, Clev.*	.278	161	587	92	163	4	51	32
Calderon, Ivan, Sea.-Chi.	.250	50	164	16	41	2	15	3
Cangelosi, John, Chi.†	.235	137	438	65	103	2	32	50
Canseco, Jose, Oak.	.240	157	600	85	144	33	117	15
Carter, Joe, Clev.	.302	162	663	108	200	29	121	29
Castillo, Carmen, Clev.	.278	85	205	34	57	8	32	2
Castillo, Juan, Milw.†	.167	26	54	6	9	0	5	1
Cerone, Rick, Milw.	.259	68	216	22	56	4	18	1
Clark, Dave, Clev.*	.276	18	59	10	16	3	9	1
Cochrane, Dave, Chi.†	.194	19	62	4	12	1	2	0
Coles, Darnell, Det.	.273	142	521	67	142	20	86	6
Collins, Dave, Det.†	.270	124	419	44	113	1	27	27
Cooper, Cecil, Milw.*	.258	134	542	46	140	12	75	1
Cotto, Henry, N.Y.	.213	35	80	11	17	1	6	3
Cowens, Al, Sea.	.183	28	82	5	15	0	6	1
Cruz, Julio, Chi.†	.215	81	209	38	45	0	19	7
Davidson, Mark, Minn	.118	36	68	5	8	0	2	2
Davis, Alvin, Sea.*	.271	135	479	66	130	18	72	0
Davis, Mike, Oak.*	.268	142	489	77	131	19	55	27
DeCinces, Doug, Cal.	.256	140	512	69	131	26	96	2
Deer, Bob, Milw.	.232	134	466	75	108	33	86	5
Dempsey, Rick, Balt.	.208	122	327	42	68	13	29	1
Downing, Brian, Cal.	.267	152	513	90	137	20	95	4
Dwyer, Jim, Balt.*	.244	94	160	18	39	8	31	0
Easler, Mike, N.Y.*	.302	146	490	64	148	14	78	3
Engle, Dave, Det.	.256	35	86	6	22	0	4	0
Espino, Juan, N.Y.	.162	27	37	1	6	0	5	0
Espinoza, Alvaro, Minn.	.214	37	42	4	9	0	1	0
Evans, Darrell, Det.*	.241	151	507	78	122	29	85	3
Evans, Dwight, Bos.	.259	152	529	86	137	26	97	3
Felder, Mike, Milw.†	.239	44	155	24	37	1	13	16
Fernandez, Tony, Tor.†	.310	163	687	91	213	10	65	25
Fielder, Cecil, Tor.	.157	34	83	7	13	4	13	0

Batter and Club	AVG	G	AB	R	H	HR	RBI	SB
Fields, Bruce, Det............	.279	16	43	4	12	0	6	1
Fischlin, Mike, N.Y.	.206	71	102	9	21	0	3	0
Fisk, Carlton, Chi.	.221	125	457	42	101	14	63	2
Fletcher, Scott, Tex.	.300	147	530	82	159	3	50	12
Foster, George, Chi.	.216	15	51	2	11	1	4	0
Franco, Julio, Clev.	.306	149	599	80	183	10	74	10
Gaetti, Gary, Minn.	.287	157	596	91	171	34	108	14
Gagne, Greg, Minn.	.250	156	472	63	118	12	54	12
Gallego, Mike, Oak.	.270	20	37	2	10	0	4	0
Gantner, Jim, Milw.*	.274	139	497	58	136	7	38	13
Garcia, Damaso, Tor........	.281	122	424	57	119	6	46	9
Gedman, Rich, Bos.*	.258	135	462	49	119	16	65	1
Gerhart, Ken, Balt.	.232	20	69	4	16	1	7	0
Gibson, Kirk, Det.*.........	.268	119	441	84	118	28	86	34
Greenwell, Mike, Bos.*	.314	31	35	4	11	0	4	0
Grich, Bobby, Cal.	.268	98	313	42	84	9	30	1
Griffey, Ken, N.Y.*	.303	59	198	33	60	9	26	2
Griffin, Alfredo, Oak.†	.285	162	594	74	169	4	51	33
Grubb, John, Det.*.........	.333	81	210	32	70	13	51	0
Gruber, Kelly, Tor.	.196	87	143	20	28	5	15	2
Guillen, Ozzie, Chi.*	.250	159	547	58	137	2	47	8
Gutierrez, Jackie, Balt......	.186	61	145	8	27	0	4	3
Hairston, Jerry, Chi.†	.271	101	225	32	61	5	26	0
Hall, Mel, Clev.*	.296	140	442	68	131	18	77	6
Harper, Brian, Det.	.139	19	36	2	5	0	3	0
Harrah, Toby, Tex.	.218	95	289	36	63	7	41	2
Hassey, Ron, N.Y.-Chi.*	.323	113	341	45	110	9	49	1
Hatcher, Mickey, Minn.	.278	115	317	40	88	3	32	2
Heath, Mike, Det.............	.265	30	98	11	26	4	11	4
Henderson, D., Sea.-Bos...	.265	139	388	59	103	15	47	2
Henderson, Rickey, N.Y.	.263	153	608	130	160	28	74	87
Hendrick, George, Cal......	.272	102	283	45	77	14	47	1
Hengel, Dave, Sea.	.190	21	63	3	12	1	6	0
Herndon, Larry, Det.	.247	106	283	33	70	8	37	2
Hill, Donnie, Oak.†	.283	108	339	37	96	4	29	5
Householder, Paul, Milw.†	.218	26	78	4	17	1	16	1
Howell, Jack, Cal.*	.272	63	151	26	41	4	21	2

Batter and Club	AVG	G	AB	R	H	HR	RBI	SB
Hrbek, Kent, Minn.*	.267	149	550	85	147	29	91	2
Hulett, Tim, Chi.	.231	150	520	53	120	17	44	4
Incaviglia, Pete, Tex.	.250	153	540	82	135	30	88	3
Iorg, Garth, Tor.	.260	137	327	30	85	3	44	3
Jackson, Bo, K.C.	.207	25	82	9	17	2	9	33
Jackson, Reggie, Cal.*	.241	132	419	65	101	18	58	1
Jacoby, Brook, Clev.	.288	158	583	83	168	17	80	2
Javier, Stan, Oak.†	.202	59	114	13	23	0	8	8
Johnson, Cliff, Tor.	.250	107	336	48	84	15	55	0
Johnson, Rondin, K.C.†	.258	11	31	1	8	0	2	0
Jones, Lynn, K.C.	.128	67	47	1	6	0	1	0
Jones, Rickie, Balt.	.182	16	33	2	6	0	4	0
Jones, Ruppert, Cal.*	.229	126	393	73	90	17	49	10
Joyner, Wally, Cal.*	.290	154	593	82	172	22	100	5
Karkovice, Ron, Chi.	.247	37	97	13	24	4	13	1
Kearney, Bob, Sea.	.240	81	204	23	49	6	25	0
Kingery, Mike, K.C.*	.258	62	209	25	54	3	14	7
Kingman, Dave, Oak.	.210	144	561	70	118	35	94	3
Kittle, Ron, Chi.-N.Y.	.218	116	376	42	82	21	60	4
Lacy, Lee, Balt.	.287	130	491	77	141	11	47	4
Laga, Mike, Det.*	.200	15	45	6	9	3	8	0
Lansford, Carney, Oak.	.284	151	591	80	168	19	72	16
Laudner, Tim, Minn.	.244	76	193	21	47	10	29	1
Law, Rudi, K.C.*	.261	87	307	42	80	1	36	14
Leach, Rick, Tor.*	.309	110	246	35	76	5	39	0
Lee, Manny, Tor.†	.205	35	78	8	16	1	7	0
Lemon, Chet, Det.	.251	126	403	45	101	12	53	2
Little, Bryan, Chi.-N.Y.†	.184	34	76	6	14	0	2	0
Lombardi, Phil, N.Y.	.278	20	36	6	10	2	6	0
Lombardozzi, Steve, Minn.	.227	156	453	53	103	8	33	3
Lowry, Dwight, Det.*	.307	56	150	21	46	3	18	0
Lynn, Fred, Balt.*	.287	112	397	67	114	23	67	2
Lyons, Steve, Bos.-Chi.*.	.227	101	247	30	56	1	20	4
Manning, Rick, Milw.*	.254	89	205	31	52	8	27	5
Martinez, Buck, Tor.	.181	81	160	13	29	2	12	0
Mattingly, Don, N.Y.*	.352	162	677	117	238	31	113	0
McDowell, Oddibe, Tex.*.	.266	154	572	105	152	18	49	33

Batter and Club	AVG	G	AB	R	H	HR	RBI	SB
McGwire, Mark, Oak.	.189	18	53	10	10	3	9	0
McRae, Hal, K.C.	.252	112	278	22	70	7	37	0
Meacham, Bobby, N.Y.†	.224	56	161	19	36	0	10	3
Mercado, Orlando, Tex.	.235	46	102	7	24	1	7	0
Miller, Darrell, Cal.	.228	33	57	6	13	0	4	0
Molitor, Paul, Milw..........	.281	105	437	62	123	9	55	20
Moore, Charlie, Milw.	.260	80	235	24	61	3	39	5
Morman, Russ, Chi.	.252	49	159	18	40	4	17	1
Moseby, Lloyd, Tor.*	.253	152	589	89	149	21	86	32
Moses, John, Sea.†........	.256	103	399	56	102	3	34	25
Motley, Darryl, K.C.	.203	72	217	22	44	7	20	0
Mulliniks, Rance, Tor.*	.259	117	348	50	90	11	45	1
Mullins, Fran, Clev..........	.175	28	40	3	7	0	5	0
Murphy, Dwayne, Oak.*	.252	98	329	50	83	9	39	3
Murray, Eddie, Balt.†.......	.305	137	495	61	151	17	84	3
Narron, Jerry, Cal.*	.221	57	95	5	21	1	8	0
Nichols, Reid, Chi.	.228	74	136	9	31	2	18	5
Nixon, Otis, Clev.†..........	.263	105	95	33	25	0	8	23
O'Brien, Pete, Tex.*	.290	156	551	86	160	23	90	4
Oglivie, Ben, Milw.*	.283	103	346	31	98	5	53	1
O'Malley, Tom, Balt.*	.254	56	181	19	46	1	18	0
Orta, Jorge, K.C.*	.277	106	336	35	93	9	46	0
Owen, Spike, Sea.-Bos.†...	.231	154	528	67	122	1	45	4
Paciorek, Tom, Tex.	.286	88	213	17	61	4	22	1
Pagliarulo, Mike, N.Y.*	.238	149	504	71	120	28	71	4
Pardo, Al, Balt.†.............	.137	16	51	3	7	1	3	0
Parrish, Lance, Det.........	.257	91	327	53	84	22	62	0
Parrish, Larry, Tex.	.276	129	464	67	128	28	94	3
Pasqua, Dan, N.Y.*	.293	102	280	44	82	16	45	2
Perconte, Jack, Chi.*	.219	24	73	6	16	0	4	2
Peters, Ricky, Oak.†........	.184	44	38	7	7	0	1	2
Petralli, Geno, Tex.†........	.255	69	137	17	35	2	18	3
Pettis, Gary, Cal.†	.258	154	539	93	139	5	58	50
Phelps, Ken, Sea.*	.247	125	344	69	85	24	64	2
Phillips, Tony, Oak.†	.256	118	441	76	113	5	52	15
Porter, Darrell, Tex.*	.265	68	155	21	41	12	29	1
Presley, Jim, Sea.	.265	155	616	83	163	27	107	0

Batter and Club	AVG	G	AB	R	H	HR	RBI	SB
Pryor, Greg, K.C.	.170	63	112	7	19	0	7	1
Puckett, Kirby, Minn.	.328	161	680	119	223	31	96	20
Quinones, Rey, Bos.-Sea.	.218	98	312	32	68	2	22	4
Quirk, Jamie, K.C.*	.215	80	219	24	47	8	26	0
Ramos, Domingo, Sea.	.182	49	99	8	18	0	5	0
Randolph, Willie, N.Y.	.276	141	492	76	136	5	50	15
Rayford, Floyd, Balt.	.176	81	210	15	37	8	19	0
Ready, Randy, Milw.	.190	23	79	8	15	1	4	2
Reed, Jeff, Minn.*	.236	68	165	13	39	2	9	1
Reynolds, Harold, Sea.†	.222	126	445	46	99	1	24	30
Rice, Jim, Bos.	.324	157	618	98	200	20	110	0
Riles, Ernest, Milw.*	.252	145	524	69	132	9	47	7
Ripken, Cal, Balt.	.282	162	627	98	177	25	81	4
Robidoux, B.J., Milw.*	.227	56	181	15	41	1	21	0
Roenicke, Gary, N.Y.	.265	69	136	11	36	3	18	1
Romero, Ed, Bos.	.210	100	233	41	49	2	23	2
Romine, Kevin, Bos.	.257	35	35	6	9	0	2	2
Ryal, Mark, Cal.*	.375	13	32	6	12	2	5	1
Sakata, Lenn, Oak.	.353	17	34	4	12	0	5	0
Salas, Mark, Minn.*	.233	91	258	28	60	8	33	3
Salazar, Angel, K.C.	.245	117	298	24	73	0	24	1
Schofield, Dick, Cal.	.249	139	458	67	114	13	57	23
Schroeder, Bill, Milw.	.212	64	217	32	46	7	19	1
Seitzer, Kevin, K.C.	.323	28	96	16	31	2	11	0
Sheets, Larry, Balt.*	.272	112	338	42	92	18	60	2
Shelby, John, Balt.†	.228	135	404	54	92	11	49	18
Shepherd, Ron, Tor.	.203	65	69	16	14	2	4	0
Sheridan, Pat, Det.*	.237	98	236	41	56	6	19	9
Sierra, Ruben, Tex.†	.264	113	382	50	101	16	55	7
Skinner, Joel, Chi.-N.Y.	.232	114	315	23	73	5	37	1
Slaught, Don, Tex.	.264	95	314	39	83	13	46	3
Smalley, Roy, Minn.†	.246	143	459	59	113	20	57	1
Smith, Lonnie, K.C.	.287	134	508	80	146	8	44	26
Snyder, Cory, Clev.	.272	103	416	58	113	24	69	2
Spilman, Harry, Det.*	.245	24	49	6	12	3	8	0
Stanley, Mike, Tex.	.333	15	30	4	10	1	1	1
Stapleton, Dave, Bos.	.128	39	39	4	5	0	3	0

Batter and Club	AVG	G	AB	R	H	HR	RBI	SB
Stefero, John, Balt.*	.233	52	120	14	28	2	13	0
Sullivan, Marc, Bos.	.193	41	119	15	23	1	14	0
Sundberg, Jim, K.C.	.212	140	429	41	91	12	42	1
Sveum, Dale, Milw.†	.246	91	317	35	78	7	35	4
Tabler, Pat, Clev.	.326	130	473	61	154	6	48	3
Tartabull, Danny, Sea.	.270	137	511	76	138	25	96	4
Tettleton, Mickey, Oak.†	.204	90	211	26	43	10	35	7
Thomas, G., Sea.-Milw.	.187	101	315	45	59	16	36	3
Thornton, Andre, Clev.	.229	120	401	49	92	17	66	4
Tillman, Rusty, Oak.	.256	22	39	6	10	1	6	2
Tolleson, W., Chi.-N.Y.†	.265	141	475	61	126	3	43	17
Tolman, Tim, Det.	.176	16	34	4	6	0	2	1
Traber, Jim, Balt.*	.255	65	212	28	54	13	44	0
Trammell, Alan, Det.	.277	151	574	107	159	21	75	25
Upshaw, Willie, Tor.*	.251	155	573	85	144	9	60	23
Valle, David, Sea.	.340	22	53	10	18	5	15	0
Walker, Greg, Chi.*	.277	78	282	37	78	13	51	1
Ward, Gary, Tex.	.316	105	380	54	120	5	51	12
Washington, C., N.Y.*	.237	54	135	19	32	6	16	6
Washington, Ron, Minn.	.257	48	74	15	19	4	11	1
Whitaker, Lou, Det.*	.269	144	584	95	157	20	73	13
White, Devon, Cal.†	.235	29	51	8	12	1	3	6
White, Frank, K.C.	.272	151	566	76	154	22	84	4
Whitt, Ernie, Tor.*	.268	131	395	48	106	16	56	0
Wiggins, Alan, Balt.†	.251	71	239	30	60	0	11	21
Wilfong, Rob, Cal.*	.219	92	288	25	63	3	33	1
Wilkerson, Curtis, Tex.†	.237	110	236	27	56	0	15	9
Willard, Jerry, Oak.*	.267	75	161	17	43	4	26	0
Williams, Kenny, Chi.	.129	15	31	2	4	1	1	1
Wilson, Willie, K.C.†	.269	156	631	77	170	9	44	34
Winfield, Dave, N.Y.	.262	154	565	90	148	24	104	6
Wright, George, Tex.†	.217	49	106	10	23	2	7	3
Wynegar, Butch, N.Y.†	.206	61	194	19	40	7	29	0
Yeager, Steve, Sea.	.208	50	130	10	27	2	12	0
Young, Mike, Balt.†	.252	117	369	43	93	9	42	3
Yount, Robin, Milw.	.312	140	522	82	163	9	46	14
Zuvella, Paul, N.Y.	.083	21	48	2	4	0	2	0

AMERICAN LEAGUE
Pitching
(85 or more innings pitched)
*Throws Lefthanded

Pitcher and Club	W	L	ERA	G	IP	H	BB	SO
Alexander, Doyle, Tor.	5	4	4.46	17	111.0	120	20	65
Allen, Neil, Chi.	7	2	3.82	22	113.0	101	38	57
Andujar, Joaquin, Oak. ...	12	7	3.82	28	155.1	139	56	72
Atherton, K., Oak.-Minn.	6	10	4.08	60	97.0	100	46	67
Bailes, Scott, Clev.*	10	10	4.95	62	112.2	123	43	60
Bankhead, Scott, K.C.	8	9	4.61	24	121.0	121	37	94
Bannister, Floyd, Chi.*	10	14	3.54	28	165.1	162	48	92
Black, Bud, K.C.*	5	10	3.20	56	121.0	100	43	68
Blyleven, Bert, Minn.......	17	14	4.01	36	271.2	262	58	215
Boddicker, Mike, Balt......	14	12	4.70	33	218.1	214	74	175
Bordi, Rich, Balt.	6	4	4.46	52	107.0	105	41	83
Boyd, Dennis, Bos.	16	10	3.78	30	214.1	222	45	129
Butcher, J., Minn.-Clev. ..	1	8	6.56	29	120.2	168	37	45
Candelaria, John, Cal.* ...	10	2	2.55	16	91.2	68	26	81
Candiotti, Tom, Clev.	16	12	3.57	36	252.1	234	106	167
Cerutti, John, Tor.*	9	4	4.15	34	145.1	150	47	89
Clancy, Jim, Tor.	14	14	3.94	34	219.1	202	63	126
Clemens, Roger, Bos.	24	4	2.48	33	254.0	179	67	238
Codiroli, Chris, Oak.	5	8	4.03	16	91.2	91	38	43
Correa, Ed, Tex.	12	14	4.23	32	202.1	167	126	189
Cowley, Joe, Chi...........	11	11	3.88	27	162.1	133	83	132
Darwin, Danny, Milw.	6	8	3.52	27	130.1	120	35	80
Davis, Joel, Chi............	4	5	4.70	19	105.1	115	51	54
Davis, Storm, Balt........	9	12	3.62	25	154.0	166	49	96
Dawley, Bill, Chi.	0	7	3.32	46	97.2	91	28	66
Dixon, Ken, Balt.	11	13	4.58	35	202.1	194	83	170
Dotson, Richard, Chi......	10	17	5.48	34	197.0	226	69	110
Drabek, Doug, N.Y.	7	8	4.10	27	131.2	126	50	76
Eichhorn, Mark, Tor.	14	6	1.72	69	157.0	105	45	166
Farr, Steve, K.C.	8	4	3.13	56	109.1	90	39	83
Fisher, Brian, N.Y.	9	5	4.93	62	96.2	105	37	67

Pitcher and Club	W	L	ERA	G	IP	H	BB	SO
Flanagan, Mike, Balt.*	7	11	4.24	29	172.0	179	66	96
Gubicza, Mark, K.C.	12	6	3.64	35	180.2	155	84	118
Guidry, Ron, N.Y.*	9	12	3.98	30	192.1	202	38	140
Guzman, Jose, Tex.	9	15	4.54	29	172.1	199	60	87
Harris, Greg, Tex.	10	8	2.83	73	111.1	103	42	95
Heaton, N., Clev.-Minn.*	7	15	4.08	33	198.2	201	81	90
Henke, Tom, Tor.	9	5	3.35	63	91.1	63	32	118
Hernandez, Willie, Det.*	8	7	3.55	64	88.2	87	21	77
Higuera, Ted, Milw.*	20	11	2.79	34	248.1	226	74	207
Hough, Charlie, Tex.	17	10	3.79	33	230.1	188	89	146
Huismann, M., K.C.-Sea.	3	4	3.79	46	97.1	98	25	72
Hurst, Bruce, Bos.*	13	8	2.99	25	174.1	169	50	167
Jackson, Danny, K.C.*	11	12	3.20	32	185.2	177	79	115
Johnson, Joe, Tor.	7	2	3.89	16	88.0	94	22	39
Key, Jimmy, Tor.*	14	11	3.57	36	232.0	222	74	141
King, Eric, Det.	11	4	3.51	33	138.1	108	63	79
Langston, Mark, Sea.*	12	14	4.85	37	239.1	234	123	245
Leary, Tim, Milw.	12	12	4.21	33	188.1	216	53	110
Leibrandt, Charlie, K.C.*	14	11	4.09	35	231.1	238	63	108
Leonard, Dennis, K.C.	8	13	4.44	33	192.2	207	51	114
Mason, Mike, Tex.*	7	3	4.33	27	135.0	135	56	85
McCaskill, Kirk, Cal.	17	10	3.36	34	246.1	207	92	202
McGregor, Scott, Balt.*	11	15	4.52	34	203.0	216	57	95
Mooneyham, Bill, Oak.	4	5	4.52	45	99.2	103	67	75
Moore, Mike, Sea.	11	13	4.30	38	266.0	279	94	146
Morgan, Mike, Sea.	11	17	4.53	37	216.1	243	86	116
Morris, Jack, Det.	21	8	3.27	35	267.0	229	82	223
Nelson, Gene, Chi.	6	6	3.85	54	114.2	118	41	70
Niekro, Joe, N.Y.	9	10	4.87	25	125.2	139	63	59
Niekro, Phil, Clev.	11	11	4.32	34	210.1	241	95	81
Nieves, Juan, Milw.*	11	12	4.92	35	184.2	224	77	116
Nipper, Al, Bos.	10	12	5.38	26	159.0	186	47	79
O'Neal, Randy, Det.	3	7	4.33	37	122.2	121	44	68
Petry, Dan, Det.	5	10	4.66	20	116.0	122	53	56
Plesac, Dan, Milw.*	10	7	2.97	51	91.0	81	29	75
Plunk, Eric, Oak.	4	7	5.31	26	120.1	91	102	98
Portugal, Mark, Minn.	6	10	4.31	27	112.2	112	50	67

94

Pitcher and Club	W	L	ERA	G	IP	H	BB	SO
Rasmussen, D., N.Y.*	18	6	3.88	31	202.0	160	74	131
Righetti, Dave, N.Y.*	8	8	2.45	74	106.2	88	35	83
Rijo, Jose, Oak.	9	11	4.65	39	193.2	172	108	176
Romanick, Ron, Cal.	5	8	5.50	18	106.1	124	44	38
Saberhagen, Bret, K.C.	7	12	4.15	30	156.0	165	29	112
Schmidt, Dave, Chi.	3	6	3.31	49	92.1	94	27	67
Schrom, Ken, Clev.	14	7	4.54	34	206.0	217	49	87
Seaver, Tom, Chi.-Bos.	7	13	4.03	28	176.1	180	56	103
Shirley, Bob, N.Y.*	0	4	5.04	39	105.1	108	40	64
Slaton, Jim, Cal.-Det.	4	6	5.08	36	113.1	130	40	43
Smithson, Mike, Minn.	13	14	4.77	34	198.0	234	57	114
Stewart, Dave, Oak.	9	5	3.74	29	149.1	137	65	102
Stieb, Dave, Tor.	7	12	4.74	37	205.0	239	87	127
Sutton, Don, Cal.	15	11	3.74	34	207.0	192	49	116
Swift, Bill, Sea.	2	9	5.46	29	115.1	148	55	55
Tanana, Frank, Det.*	12	9	4.16	32	188.1	196	65	119
Terrell, Walt, Det.	15	12	4.56	34	217.1	199	98	93
Tewksbury, Bob, N.Y.	9	5	3.31	23	130.1	144	31	49
Viola, Frank, Minn.*	16	13	4.51	37	245.2	257	83	191
Wegman, Bill, Milw.	5	12	5.13	35	198.1	217	43	82
Williams, Mitch, Tex.*	8	6	3.58	80	98.0	69	79	90
Witt, Bobby, Tex.	11	9	5.48	31	157.2	130	143	174
Witt, Mike, Cal.	18	10	2.84	34	269.0	218	73	208
Young, Curt, Oak.*	13	9	3.45	29	198.0	176	57	116
Young, Matt, Sea.*	8	6	3.82	65	103.2	108	46	82

NATIONAL LEAGUE
Batting

(40 or more at-bats)
*Bats Lefthanded   †Switch-Hitter

Batter and Club	AVG	G	AB	R	H	HR	RBI	SB
Aguayo, Luis, Phil.	.211	62	133	17	28	4	13	1
Aguilera, Richard, N.Y.	.157	32	51	4	8	2	6	0
Aldrete, Michael, S.F.*	.250	84	216	27	54	2	25	1
Almon, William, Pitt.	.219	102	196	29	43	7	27	11
Anderson, David, L.A.	.245	92	216	31	53	1	15	5
Asadoor, Randall, S.D.	.364	15	55	9	20	0	7	1
Ashby, Alan, Hou.†	.257	120	315	24	81	7	38	1
Backman, Walter, N.Y.†	.320	124	387	67	124	1	27	13
Bailey, J. Mark, Hou.†	.176	57	153	9	27	4	15	1
Bass, Kevin, Hou.†	.311	157	591	83	184	20	79	22
Bell, David, Cin.	.278	155	568	89	158	20	75	2
Belliard, Rafael, Pitt.	.233	117	309	33	72	0	31	12
Benedict, Bruce, Atl.	.225	64	160	11	36	0	13	1
Bielecki, Michael, Pitt.	.063	31	48	3	3	0	1	0
Bilardello, Dann, Mtl.	.194	79	191	12	37	4	17	1
Blue, Vida, S.F.†	.093	28	43	3	4	1	3	0
Bochy, Bruce, S.D.	.252	63	127	16	32	8	22	1
Bonds, Barry, Pitt.*	.223	113	413	72	92	16	48	36
Bonilla, Roberto, Pitt.†	.240	63	192	28	46	1	17	4
Bosley, Thaddis, Chi.*	.275	87	120	15	33	1	9	3
Bream, Sidney, Pitt.*	.268	154	522	73	140	16	77	13
Brenly, Robert, S.F.	.246	149	472	60	116	16	62	10
Brock, Gregory, L.A.*	.234	115	325	33	76	16	52	2
Brooks, Hubert, Mtl.	.340	80	306	50	104	14	58	4
Brown, J. Christopher, S.F.	.317	116	416	57	132	7	49	13
Brown, Michael C., Pitt.	.218	87	243	18	53	4	26	2
Browning, Thomas, Cin.*	.163	46	86	9	14	0	3	1
Bryant, Ralph, L.A.*	.253	27	75	15	19	6	13	0
Butera, Salvatore, Cin.	.239	56	113	14	27	2	16	0
Cabell, Enos, L.A.	.256	107	277	27	71	2	29	10
Candaele, Casey, Mtl.†	.230	30	104	9	24	0	6	3

Batter and Club	AVG	G	AB	R	H	HR	RBI	SB
Carlton, Steven, Phil.-S.F.*	.200	22	45	4	9	1	8	0
Carter, Gary, N.Y.	.255	132	490	81	125	24	105	1
Cedeno, Cesar, L.A.	.231	37	78	5	18	0	6	1
Cey, Ronald, Chi.	.273	97	256	42	70	13	36	0
Chambliss, Chris, Atl.*	.311	97	122	13	38	2	14	0
Clark, Jack, St.L.	.237	65	232	34	55	9	23	1
Clark, William, S.F.*	.287	111	408	66	117	11	41	4
Coleman, Vincent, St. L.†	.232	154	600	94	139	0	29	107
Concepcion, David, Cin.	.260	90	311	42	81	3	30	13
Cox, Danny, St.L.	.077	32	65	2	5	0	2	0
Cruz, Jose, Hou.*	.278	141	479	48	133	10	72	3
Daniels, Kalvoski, Cin.*	.320	74	181	34	58	6	23	15
Darling, Ronald, N.Y.	.099	34	81	4	8	0	0	0
Daulton, Darren, Phil.*	.225	49	138	18	31	8	21	2
Davis, Charles, S.F.†	.278	153	526	71	146	13	70	16
Davis, Eric, Cin.	.277	132	415	97	115	27	71	80
Davis, Glenn, Hou.	.265	158	574	91	152	31	101	3
Davis, Jody, Chi.	.250	148	528	61	132	21	74	0
Dawson, Andre, Mtl.	.284	130	496	65	141	20	78	18
Dayett, Brian, Chi.	.269	24	67	7	18	4	11	0
Denny, John, Cin.	.222	27	54	6	12	0	4	2
Dernier, Robert, Chi.	.225	108	324	32	73	4	18	27
Deshaies, James, Hou.*	.047	26	43	3	2	0	1	0
Diaz, Baudilio, Cin.	.272	134	474	50	129	10	56	1
Diaz, Michael, Pitt.	.268	97	209	22	56	12	36	0
Doran, William, Hou.†	.276	145	550	92	152	6	37	42
Dravecky, David, S.D.	.140	35	50	3	7	1	7	1
Duncan, Mariano, L.A.† ...	.229	109	407	47	93	8	30	48
Dunston, Shawon, Chi.	.250	150	581	66	145	17	68	13
Durham, Leon, Chi.*	.262	141	484	66	127	20	65	8
Dykstra, Leonard, N.Y.* ...	.295	147	431	77	127	8	45	31
Eckersley, Dennis, Chi.	.159	33	69	7	11	2	10	0
Esasky, Nicholas, Cin.	.230	102	330	35	76	12	41	0
Fernandez, C. Sid., N.Y.* ...	.162	32	68	6	11	0	4	1
Fitzgerald, Michael, Mtl.	.282	73	209	20	59	6	37	3
Flannery, Timothy, S.D.* ...	.280	134	368	48	103	3	28	3
Foley, Thomas, Phil.-Mtl.*	.266	103	263	26	70	1	23	10

Batter and Club	AVG	G	AB	R	H	HR	RBI	SB
Ford, Curtis, St.L.*	.248	85	214	30	53	2	29	13
Forsch, Robert, St.L.	.171	34	76	7	13	2	12	0
Foster, George, N.Y.	.227	72	233	28	53	13	38	1
Francona, Terry, Chi.*	.250	86	124	13	31	2	8	0
Gainey, Telmanch, Hou.*	.300	26	50	6	15	1	6	3
Galarraga, Andres, Mtl.	.271	105	321	39	87	10	42	6
Garner, Philip, Hou.	.265	107	313	43	83	9	41	12
Garrelts, Scott, S.F.	.178	54	45	6	8	1	4	1
Garvey, Steven, S.D.	.255	155	557	58	142	21	81	1
Gladden, C. Daniel, S.F.	.276	102	351	55	97	4	29	27
Gonzalez, Jose, L.A.	.215	57	93	15	20	2	6	4
Gooden, Dwight, N.Y.	.086	33	81	5	7	0	4	0
Griffey, G. Kenneth, Atl.*	.308	80	292	36	90	12	32	12
Gross, Gregory, Phil.*	.248	87	101	11	25	0	8	1
Gross, Kevin, Phil.	.188	37	80	6	15	1	5	1
Guerrero, Pedro, L.A.	.246	31	61	7	15	5	10	0
Gullickson, William, Cin.	.076	37	79	3	6	0	2	0
Gwynn, Anthony, S.D.*	.329	160	642	107	211	14	59	37
Hall, Albert, Atl.†	.240	16	50	6	12	0	1	8
Hamilton, Jeffrey, L.A.	.224	71	147	22	33	5	19	0
Harper, Terry, Atl.	.257	106	265	26	68	8	30	3
Hatcher, William, Hou.	.258	127	419	55	108	6	36	38
Hawkins, M. Andrew, S.D.	.149	37	67	2	10	0	2	0
Hayes, Von, Phil.*	.305	158	610	107	186	19	98	24
Hearn, Edward, N.Y.	.265	49	136	16	36	4	10	0
Heath, Michael, St.L.	.205	65	190	19	39	4	25	2
Heep, Daniel, N.Y.*	.282	86	195	24	55	5	33	1
Hernandez, Keith, N.Y.*	.310	149	551	94	171	13	83	2
Herr, Thomas, St.L.†	.252	152	559	48	141	2	61	22
Hershiser, Orel, L.A.	.239	37	71	4	17	0	8	0
Honeycutt, Fred., L.A.*	.070	32	43	3	3	0	3	0
Horner, J. Robert, Atl.	.273	141	517	70	141	27	87	1
Hoyt, D. LaMarr, S.D.	.130	35	46	3	6	0	1	0
Hubbard, Glenn, Atl.	.230	143	408	42	94	4	36	3
Hudson, Charles, Phil.	.047	36	43	2	2	0	0	0
Hunt, J. Randall, Mtl.	.208	21	48	4	10	2	5	0
Hurdle, Clinton, St.L.*	.195	78	154	18	30	3	15	0

Batter and Club	AVG	G	AB	R	H	HR	RBI	SB
Iorg, Dane, S.D.*	.226	90	106	10	24	2	11	0
James, D. Chris., Phil.	.283	16	46	5	13	1	5	0
Jeltz, L. Steven, Phil.†	.219	145	439	44	96	0	36	6
Johnson, Howard, N.Y.†	.245	88	220	30	54	10	39	8
Johnson, Wallace, Mtl.†	.283	61	127	13	36	1	10	6
Jones, Tracy, Cin............	.349	46	86	16	30	2	10	7
Kennedy, Terrence, S.D.* ...	.264	141	432	46	114	12	57	0
Khalifa, Sam, Pitt............	.185	64	151	8	28	0	4	0
Knepper, Robert, Hou.*	.099	42	91	2	9	0	1	0
Knicely, Alan, St. L.	.195	34	82	8	16	1	6	1
Knight, C. Ray, N.Y.........	.298	137	486	51	145	11	76	2
Krenchicki, Wayne, Mtl.* ...	.240	101	221	21	53	2	23	2
Kruk, John, S.D.*	.309	122	278	33	86	4	38	2
Krukow, Michael, S.F.	.146	35	82	7	12	0	8	1
Kutcher, Randy, S.F.	.237	71	186	28	44	7	16	6
LaCoss, Michael, S.F.	.230	37	61	8	14	2	9	0
Laga, Michael, St. L.*	.217	18	46	7	10	3	8	0
Lake, Steven, Chi.-St. L. ...	.294	36	68	8	20	2	14	0
Landreaux, Ken., L.A.*	.261	103	283	34	74	4	29	10
Landrum, Terry, St. L.	.210	96	205	24	43	2	17	3
Larkin, Barry, Cin...........	.283	41	159	27	45	3	19	8
LaValliere, Michael, St.L.*	.234	110	303	18	71	3	30	0
Law, Vance, Mtl.............	.225	112	360	37	81	5	44	3
Leonard, Jeffrey, S.F.	.279	89	341	48	95	6	42	16
Lindeman, James, St.L.	.255	19	55	7	14	1	6	1
Lopes, David, Chi.-Hou.....	.275	96	255	49	70	7	35	25
Madlock, Bill, L.A.	.280	111	379	38	106	10	60	3
Mahler, Richard, Atl.	.193	40	83	8	16	0	7	0
Maldonado, Candido, S.F.	.252	133	405	49	102	18	85	4
Marshall, Michael, L.A.....	.233	103	330	47	77	19	53	4
Martinez, Carmelo, S.D....	.238	113	244	28	58	9	25	1
Martinez, David, Chi.*	.139	53	108	13	15	1	7	4
Mathews, Gregory, St.L.†	.047	23	43	1	2	0	2	0
Matthews, Gary, Chi.	.259	123	370	49	96	21	46	3
Matuszek, Leonard, L.A.*	.261	91	199	26	52	9	28	2
Mazzilli, Lee, Pitt.-N.Y.† ...	.245	100	151	28	37	3	15	4
McGee, Willie, St.L.	.256	124	497	65	127	7	48	19

Batter and Club	AVG	G	AB	R	H	HR	RBI	SB
McReynolds, W. K., S.D.	.288	158	560	89	161	26	96	8
Melvin, Robert, S.F.	.224	89	268	24	60	5	25	3
Milner, Eddie, Cin.*	.259	145	424	70	110	15	47	18
Mitchell, Kevin, N.Y.	.277	108	328	51	91	12	43	3
Mizerock, John, Hou.*	.185	44	81	9	15	1	6	0
Moreland, B. Keith, Chi.	.271	156	586	72	159	12	79	3
Moreno, Omar, Atl.*	.234	118	359	46	84	4	27	17
Morris, John, St.L.*	.240	39	100	8	24	1	14	6
Morrison, James, Pitt.	.274	154	537	58	147	23	88	9
Mumphrey, Jerry, Chi.†	.304	111	309	37	94	5	32	2
Murphy, Dale, Atl.	.265	160	614	89	163	29	83	7
Nettles, Graig, S.D.*	.218	126	354	36	77	16	55	0
Newman, Albert, Mtl.†	.200	95	185	23	37	1	8	11
Niedenfuer, Thomas, L.A.	.500	60	4	1	2	0	2	0
Nieto, Thomas, Mtl.	.200	30	65	5	13	1	7	0
Oberkfell, Kenneth, Atl.*	.270	151	503	62	136	5	48	7
Oester, Ronald, Cin.†	.258	153	523	52	135	8	44	9
Ojeda, Robert, N.Y.*	.113	32	71	3	8	0	0	0
Oquendo, Jose, St.L.†	.297	76	138	20	41	0	13	2
Orsulak, Joseph, Pitt.*	.249	138	401	60	100	2	19	24
Ortiz, Adalberto, Pitt.	.336	49	110	11	37	0	14	0
Palmeiro, Rafael, Chi.*	.247	22	73	9	18	3	12	1
Palmer, David, Atl.	.182	35	66	3	12	1	6	0
Pankovits, James, Hou.	.283	70	113	12	32	1	7	1
Parker, David, Cin.*	.273	162	637	89	174	31	116	1
Pena, Antonio, Pitt.	.288	144	510	56	147	10	52	9
Pendleton, Terry, St.L.†	.239	159	578	56	138	1	59	24
Perez, Atanasio, Cin.	.255	77	200	14	51	2	29	0
Perry, Gerald, Atl.*	.271	29	70	6	19	2	11	0
Puhl, Terrance, Hou.*	.244	81	172	17	42	3	14	3
Pyznarski, Timothy, S.D.	.238	15	42	3	10	0	0	2
Quinones, Luis, S.F.†	.179	71	106	13	19	0	11	3
Raines, Timothy, Mtl.†	.334	151	580	91	194	9	62	70
Ramirez, Rafael, Atl.	.240	134	496	57	119	8	33	19
Rawley, Shane, Phil.	.173	23	52	5	9	0	1	0
Ray, Johnny, Pitt.†	.301	155	579	67	174	7	78	6
Redus, Gary, Phil.	.247	90	340	62	84	11	33	25

Batter and Club	AVG	G	AB	R	H	HR	RBI	SB
Reuschel, Ricky, Pitt.	.157	43	70	7	11	0	6	0
Reynolds, G. Craig, Hou.*	.249	114	313	32	78	6	41	3
Reynolds, Robert, Pitt.†	.269	118	402	63	108	9	48	16
Reynolds, Ronn, Phil.	.214	43	126	8	27	3	10	0
Rhoden, Richard, Pitt.	.278	41	90	9	25	1	10	0
Rivera, Luis, Mtl.	.205	55	166	20	34	0	13	1
Roberts, Leon, S.D.†	.253	101	241	34	61	1	12	14
Roenicke, Ronald, Phil.†	.247	102	275	42	68	5	42	2
Rose, Peter, Cin.†	.219	72	237	15	52	0	25	3
Rowdon, Wade, Cin.	.250	38	80	9	20	0	10	2
Royster, Jeron, S.D.	.257	118	257	31	66	5	26	3
Ruffin, Bruce, Phil.	.073	21	55	2	4	0	2	0
Russell, John, Phil.	.241	93	315	35	76	13	60	0
Russell, William, L.A.	.250	105	216	21	54	0	18	7
Ryan, L. Nolan, Hou.	.102	30	59	1	6	0	5	0
Sample, William, Atl.	.285	92	200	23	57	6	14	4
Samuel, Juan, Phil.	.266	145	591	90	157	16	78	42
Sandberg, Ryne, Chi.	.284	154	627	68	178	14	76	34
Sanderson, Scott, Chi.	.059	38	51	1	3	0	2	0
Santana, Rafael, N.Y.	.218	139	394	38	86	1	28	0
Santiago, Benito, S.D.	.290	17	62	10	18	3	6	0
Sax, Stephen, L.A.	.332	157	633	91	210	6	56	40
Schmidt, Michael, Phil.	.290	160	552	97	160	37	119	1
Schu, Richard, Phil.	.274	92	208	32	57	8	25	2
Scioscia, Michael, L.A.*	.251	122	374	36	94	5	26	3
Scott, Michael, Hou.	.126	38	95	7	12	0	3	0
Show, Eric, S.D.	.163	24	43	2	7	0	1	0
Simmons, Ted, Atl.†	.252	76	127	14	32	4	25	1
Smith, Bryn, Mtl.	.138	30	58	3	8	1	7	0
Smith, Osborne, St.L.†	.280	153	514	67	144	0	54	31
Smith, Zane, Atl.*	.085	43	59	2	5	0	3	0
Speier, Chris, Chi.	.284	95	155	21	44	6	23	2
Spilman, W. Harry, S.F.*	.287	58	94	12	27	2	22	0
Stillwell, Kurt, Cin.†	.229	104	279	31	64	0	26	6
Stone, Jeffrey, Phil.*	.277	82	249	32	69	6	19	19
Strawberry, Darryl, N.Y.*	.259	136	475	76	123	27	93	28
Stubbs, Franklin, L.A.*	.226	132	420	55	95	23	58	7

Batter and Club	AVG	G	AB	R	H	HR	RBI	SB
Sutcliffe, Richard, Chi.*	.208	29	53	3	11	1	4	0
Templeton, Garry, S.D.†	.247	147	510	42	126	2	44	10
Teufel, Timothy, N.Y.	.247	93	279	35	69	4	31	1
Thomas, Andres, Atl.	.251	102	323	26	81	6	32	4
Thompson, Jason, Mtl.*	.196	30	51	6	10	0	4	0
Thompson, Milton, Phil.*	.251	96	299	38	75	6	23	19
Thompson, Robert, S.F.	.271	149	549	73	149	7	47	12
Thon, Richard, Hou.	.248	106	278	24	69	3	21	6
Tibbs, Jay, Mtl.	.130	36	54	2	7	0	0	0
Trevino, Alejandro, L.A.	.262	89	202	31	53	4	26	0
Trillo, J. Manuel, Chi.	.296	81	152	22	45	1	19	0
Trout, Steven, Chi.*	.209	37	43	5	9	0	3	0
Tudor, John, St.L.*	.153	30	72	6	11	0	6	0
Uribe, Jose, S.F.†	.223	157	453	46	101	3	43	22
Valenzuela, F., L.A.*	.220	39	109	5	24	0	7	0
Van Slyke, Andrew, St.L.*	.270	137	418	48	113	13	61	21
Venable, W. M., Cin.*	.211	108	147	17	31	2	15	7
Virgil, Osvaldo, Atl.	.223	114	359	45	80	15	48	1
Walker, Anthony, Hou.	.222	84	90	19	20	2	10	11
Walker, Cleotha, Chi.†	.277	28	101	21	28	1	7	15
Wallach, Timothy, Mtl.	.233	134	480	50	112	18	71	8
Walling, Dennis, Hou.*	.312	130	382	54	119	13	58	1
Washington, C., Atl*	.270	40	137	17	37	5	14	4
Washington, U.L., Pitt.†	.200	72	135	14	27	0	10	6
Webster, Mitchell, Mtl.†	.290	151	576	89	167	8	49	36
Welch, Robert, L.A.	.105	35	76	2	8	1	4	0
Welsh, Chris., Cin.*	.119	24	42	3	5	1	4	1
Williams, Reg., L.A.	.277	128	303	35	84	4	32	9
Wilson, Glenn, Phil.	.271	155	584	70	158	15	84	5
Wilson, William, N.Y.†	.289	123	381	61	110	9	45	25
Winningham, H., Mtl.*	.216	90	185	23	40	4	11	12
Wohlford, James, Mtl.	.266	70	94	10	25	1	11	0
Woodard, Michael, S.F.*	.253	48	79	14	20	1	5	7
Wright, George, Mtl.†	.188	56	117	12	22	0	5	1
Wynne, Marvell, S.D.*	.264	137	288	34	76	7	37	11
Youmans, Floyd, Mtl.	.160	33	75	4	12	1	7	0
Youngblood, Joel, S.F.	.255	97	184	20	47	5	28	1

(40 or more innings pitched)
*Throws Lefthanded

Pitcher and Club	W	L	ERA	G	IP	H	BB	SO
Acker, James, Atl.	3	8	3.79	21	95.0	100	26	37
Aguilera, Richard, N.Y. ...	10	7	3.88	28	141.2	145	36	104
Alexander, Doyle, Atl.	6	6	3.84	17	117.1	135	17	74
Andersen, L., Phil.-Hou.	2	1	3.03	48	77.1	83	26	42
Anderson, Richard, N.Y. ...	2	1	2.72	15	49.2	45	11	21
Assenmacher, Paul, Atl.*	7	3	2.50	61	68.1	61	26	56
Baller, Jay, Chi.	2	4	5.37	36	53.2	58	28	42
Bedrosian, Stephen, Phil.	8	6	3.39	68	90.1	79	34	82
Berenguer, Juan, S.F.......	2	3	2.70	46	73.1	64	44	72
Berenyi, Bruce, N.Y........	2	2	6.35	14	39.2	47	22	30
Bielecki, Michael, Pitt.	6	11	4.66	31	148.2	149	83	83
Blue, Vida, S.F.*	10	10	3.27	28	156.2	137	77	100
Browning, Thomas, Cin.*	14	13	3.81	39	243.1	225	70	147
Burke, Timothy, Mtl.	9	7	2.93	68	101.1	103	46	82
Burris, B. Ray, St.L.	4	5	5.60	23	82.0	92	32	34
Carlton, S., Phil.-S.F.* ...	5	11	5.89	22	113.0	138	61	80
Carman, Donald, Phil.* ...	10	5	3.22	50	134.1	113	52	98
Clements, Pat., Pitt.*	0	4	2.80	65	61.0	53	32	31
Conroy, Timothy, St.L.* ..	5	11	5.23	25	115.1	122	56	79
Cox, Danny, St.L.	12	13	2.90	32	220.0	189	60	108
Darling, Ronald, N.Y.	15	6	2.81	34	237.0	203	81	184
Darwin, Danny, Hou.......	5	2	2.32	12	54.1	50	9	40
Davis, Mark, S.F.*.........	5	7	2.99	67	84.1	63	34	90
Dayley, Kenneth, St.L.*...	0	3	3.26	31	38.2	42	11	33
Dedmon, Jeffrey, Atl.	6	6	2.98	57	99.2	90	39	58
Denny, John, Cin.	11	10	4.20	27	171.1	179	56	115
Deshaies, James, Hou.* ..	12	5	3.25	26	144.0	124	59	128
DiPino, Frank, Hou.-Chi.*	3	7	4.37	61	80.1	74	30	70
Downs, Kelly, S.F.	4	4	2.75	14	88.1	78	30	64
Dravecky, David, S.D.* ...	9	11	3.07	26	161.1	149	54	87

Pitcher and Club	W	L	ERA	G	IP	H	BB	SO
Eckersley, Dennis, Chi. ...	6	11	4.57	33	201.0	226	43	137
Fernandez, C. Sid., N.Y.*	16	6	3.52	32	204.1	161	91	200
Fontenot, S. Ray, Chi.* ...	3	5	3.86	42	56.0	57	21	24
Forsch, Robert, St.L.	14	10	3.25	33	230.0	211	68	104
Franco, John, Cin.*	6	6	2.94	74	101.0	90	44	84
Frazier, George, Chi.	2	4	5.40	35	51.2	63	34	41
Garber, H. Eugene, Atl. ...	5	5	2.54	61	78.0	76	20	56
Garrelts, Scott, S.F.	13	9	3.11	53	173.2	144	74	125
Gooden, Dwight, N.Y.	17	6	2.84	33	250.0	197	80	200
Gossage, Richard, S.D. ..	5	7	4.45	45	64.2	69	20	63
Gross, Kevin, Phil.	12	12	4.02	37	241.2	240	94	154
Guante, Cecilio, Pitt.	5	2	3.35	52	78.0	65	29	63
Gullickson, W., Cin.	15	12	3.38	37	244.2	245	60	121
Gumpert, David, Chi.	2	0	4.37	38	59.2	60	28	45
Hawkins, M.A., S.D.	10	8	4.30	37	209.1	218	75	117
Hershiser, Orel, L.A.	14	14	3.85	35	231.1	213	86	153
Hesketh, Joseph, Mtl.* ...	6	5	5.01	15	82.2	92	31	67
Hoffman, Guy, Chi.*	6	2	3.86	32	84.0	92	29	47
Honeycutt, F., L.A.*	11	9	3.32	32	171.0	164	45	100
Horton, Ricky, St.L.*	4	3	2.24	42	100.1	77	26	49
Howell, Kenneth, L.A.	6	12	3.87	62	97.2	86	63	104
Hoyt, D. LaMarr, S.D.	8	11	5.15	35	159.0	170	68	85
Hudson, Charles, Phil.....	7	10	4.94	33	144.0	165	58	82
Hume, Thomas, Phil.	4	1	2.77	48	94.1	89	34	51
Johnson, Joseph, Atl.	6	7	4.97	17	87.0	101	35	49
Jones, Barry, Pitt.	3	4	2.89	26	37.1	29	21	29
Keough, M., Chi.-Hou. ...	5	4	3.94	29	64.0	58	30	44
Kerfeld, Charles, Hou.	11	2	2.59	61	93.2	71	42	77
Kipper, Robert, Pitt.*	6	8	4.03	20	114.0	123	34	81
Knepper, Robert, Hou.*...	17	12	3.14	40	258.0	232	62	143
Knudson, Mark, Hou......	1	5	4.22	9	42.2	48	15	20
Krukow, Michael, S.F.	20	9	3.05	34	245.0	204	55	178
LaCoss, Michael, S.F.	10	13	3.57	37	204.1	179	70	86
LaPoint, David, S.D.*	1	4	4.26	24	61.1	67	24	41
Lefferts, Craig, S.D.*	9	8	3.09	83	107.2	98	44	72
Lopez, Aurelio, Hou.	3	3	3.46	45	78.0	64	25	44
Lynch, Edward, N.Y.-Chi.	7	5	3.73	24	101.1	107	23	58

Pitcher and Club	W	L	ERA	G	IP	H	BB	SO
Madden, Michael, Hou.*..	1	2	4.08	13	39.2	47	22	30
Maddux, Gregory, Chi.....	2	4	5.52	6	31.0	44	11	20
Maddux, Michael, Phil. ...	3	7	5.42	16	78.0	88	34	44
Mahler, Richard, Atl. 14		18	4.88	39	237.2	283	95	137
Martinez, Dennis, Mtl.	3	6	4.59	19	98.0	103	28	63
Mason, Roger, S.F.	3	4	4.80	11	60.0	56	30	43
Mathews, Gregory, St.L.*11		8	3.65	23	145.1	139	44	67
McClure, Robert, Mtl.* ...	2	5	3.02	52	62.2	53	23	42
McCullers, Lance, S.D....10		10	2.78	70	136.0	103	58	92
McDowell, Roger, N.Y. ...14		9	3.02	75	128.0	107	42	65
McGaffigan, A., Mtl. 10		5	2.65	48	142.2	114	55	104
McMurtry, J. Craig, Atl. ...	1	6	4.74	37	79.2	82	43	50
McWilliams, Larry, Pitt.*	3	11	5.15	49	122.1	129	49	80
Minton, Gregory, S.F.	4	4	3.93	48	68.2	63	34	34
Moyer, Jamie, Chi.*.......	7	4	5.05	16	87.1	107	42	45
Mulholland, T., S.F.*	1	7	4.94	15	54.2	51	35	27
Murphy, Robert, Cin.*	6	0	0.72	34	50.1	26	21	36
Niedenfuer, Thomas, L.A.	6	6	3.71	60	80.0	86	29	55
Niemann, Randy, N.Y.* ...	2	3	3.79	31	35.2	44	12	18
Ojeda, Robert, N.Y.* 18		5	2.57	32	217.1	185	52	148
Olwine, Edward, Atl.*.....	0	0	3.40	37	47.2	35	17	37
Orosco, Jesse, N.Y.	8	6	2.33	58	81.0	64	35	62
Ownbey, Richard, St.L....	1	3	3.80	17	42.2	47	19	25
Palmer, David, Atl. 11		10	3.65	35	209.2	181	102	170
Patterson, Bob, Pitt.*.....	2	3	4.95	11	36.1	49	5	20
Pena, Alejandro, L.A.	1	2	4.89	24	70.0	74	30	46
Perry, W. Patrick, St.L.*	2	3	3.80	46	68.2	59	34	29
Powell, Dennis, L.A.*.....	2	7	4.27	27	65.1	65	25	31
Power, Ted, Cin. 10		6	3.70	56	129.0	115	52	95
Price, Joseph, Cin.*	1	2	5.40	25	41.2	49	22	30
Rawley, Shane, Phil.*.....11		7	3.54	23	157.2	166	50	73
Reardon, Jeffrey, Mtl......	7	9	3.94	62	89.0	83	26	67
Reuschel, Ricky, Pitt.	9	16	3.96	35	215.2	232	57	125
Reuss, Jerry, L.A.*	2	6	5.84	19	74.0	96	17	29
Rhoden, Richard, Pitt. 15		12	2.84	34	253.2	211	76	159
Robinson, Don, Pitt.	3	4	3.38	50	69.1	61	27	53
Robinson, Jeffrey, S.F.	6	3	3.36	64	104.1	92	32	90

Pitcher and Club	W	L	ERA	G	IP	H	BB	SO
Robinson, Ronald, Cin.	10	3	3.24	70	116.2	110	43	117
Ruffin, Bruce, Phil.*	9	4	2.46	21	146.1	138	44	70
Ryan, L. Nolan, Hou.	12	8	3.34	30	178.0	119	82	194
Sanderson, Scott, Chi.	9	11	4.19	37	169.2	165	37	124
Schatzeder, D., Mtl.-Phil.*	6	5	3.26	55	88.1	81	35	47
Scott, Michael, Hou.	18	10	2.22	37	275.1	182	72	306
Sebra, Robert, Mtl.	5	5	3.55	17	91.1	82	25	66
Show, Eric, S.D.	9	5	2.97	24	136.1	109	69	94
Sisk, Douglas, N.Y.	4	2	3.06	41	70.2	77	31	31
Smith, Bryn, Mtl.	10	8	3.94	30	187.1	182	63	105
Smith, David, Hou.	4	7	2.73	54	56.0	39	22	46
Smith, Lee, Chi.	9	9	3.09	66	90.1	69	42	93
Smith, Zane, Atl.*	8	16	4.05	38	204.2	209	105	139
Soff, Raymond, St.L.	4	2	3.29	30	38.1	37	13	22
Solano, Julio, Hou.	3	1	7.59	16	32.0	39	22	21
Soto, Mario, Cin.	5	10	4.71	19	105.0	113	46	67
Stoddard, Timothy, S.D.	1	3	3.77	30	45.1	33	34	47
Sutcliffe, Richard, Chi.	5	14	4.64	28	176.2	166	96	122
Tekulve, Kenton, Phil.	11	5	2.54	73	110.0	99	25	57
Terry, Scott, Cin.	1	2	6.14	28	55.2	66	32	32
Thurmond, Mark, S.D.*	3	7	6.50	17	70.2	96	27	32
Tibbs, Jay, Mtl.	7	9	3.97	35	190.1	181	70	117
Trout, Steven, Chi.*	5	7	4.75	37	161.0	184	78	69
Tudor, John, St.L.*	13	7	2.92	30	219.0	197	53	107
Valenzuela, F., L.A.*	21	11	3.14	34	269.1	226	85	242
Vande Berg, Edward, L.A.*	1	5	3.41	60	71.1	83	33	42
Walk, Robert, Pitt.	7	8	3.75	44	141.2	129	64	78
Walter, Gene, S.D.*	2	2	3.86	57	98.0	89	49	84
Welch, Robert, L.A.	7	13	3.28	33	235.2	227	55	183
Welsh, Chris., Cin.*	6	9	4.78	24	139.1	163	40	40
Whitson, Eddie, S.D.	1	7	5.59	17	75.2	85	37	46
Williams, Frank, S.F.	3	1	1.20	36	52.1	35	21	33
Willis, Carl, Cin.	1	3	4.47	29	52.1	54	32	24
Winn, James, Pitt.	3	5	3.58	50	88.0	85	38	70
Wojna, Edward, S.D.	2	2	3.23	7	39.0	42	16	19
Worrell, Todd, St.L.	9	10	2.08	74	103.2	86	41	73
Youmans, Floyd, Mtl.	13	12	3.53	33	219.0	145	118	202

BRUCE WEBER PICKS
HOW THEY'LL FINISH IN 1987

American League East

1. Toronto
2. New York
3. Boston
4. Cleveland
5. Detroit
6. Baltimore
7. Milwaukee

American League West

1. Texas
2. Oakland
3. Kansas City
4. Minnesota
5. California
6. Chicago
7. Seattle

National League East

1. New York
2. Philadelphia
3. St. Louis
4. Chicago
5. Monteal
6. Pittsburgh

National League West

1. Cincinnati
2. San Francisco
3. Houston
4. Los Angeles
5. Atlanta
6. San Diego

American League Champions: Toronto Blue Jays

National League Champions: New York Mets

World Champions: New York Mets

YOU PICK
HOW THEY'LL FINISH IN 1987

**American League
East**

1.

2.

3.

4.

5.

6.

7.

**American League
West**

1.

2.

3.

4.

5.

6.

7.

**National League
East**

1.

2.

3.

4.

5.

6.

**National League
West**

1.

2.

3.

4.

5.

6.

American League Champions:

National League Champions:

World Champions: